Managing from Clarity

Managing from Clarity

Identifying, Aligning and Leveraging Strategic Resources

James L. Ritchie-Dunham

and

Hal T. Rabbino

JOHN WILEY & SONS, LTD
Chichester · New York · Weinheim · Brisbane · Singapore · Toronto

JLRD To Leslie, the spark of my existence.
To the giants on whose shoulders we stand.

HTR To Luzma, my north and light of my path.
To my partners, for filling the journey with new challenges,
clear purpose and genuine laughter.

Contents

Managing from Clarity

'This approach ... [changes] the way leaders think, enabling them to literally "get their mind around the business" and the complexities facing it.'
R. *Scott Spann, VP Operations, Consilient*

'The GRASP methodology gave me great clarity about my organization's internal processes, structures, resources, people's goals and objectives, how they all interrelate, and which actions were the most important. This vision will change how business is done in the future.'
Jorge Lozano Dubernard, former Director of Strategic Planning, Banca Serfin; CEO Max Marketing

'Having worked with Ritchie-Dunham and Rabbino in real world situations, I can say that no one is better at helping organizations translate the theory into useful practice.'
Jay Weiss, Vice President, Sagebrush Wireless Holdings, LLC

'an indispensable tool for enabling strategists and decision makers to manage from clarity ... a fine treatment of a difficult subject.'
Hans-Peter von Sicard, Executive Vice President, Emergence Consulting, former VP of Practice Development in Renaissance Worldwide

'The *Managing from Clarity* process enables business leaders to "get their mind around" the dynamic, multi-faceted system that **is** their enterprise.'
H. Dan Farell, President, Distribution, TXU Electric & Gas

'The process and tools provided us a practical and effective way to get our group and its goals aligned around what really matters for our organization as a whole.'
Elizabeth Martínez, Senior Vice President, Department of Structured Finance, Banco Nacional de México

'Decision-making . . . was made clearer by considering strategic and non-technical issues.'
T.H. van der Harst, organizer, project framing workshop,
Shell International Exploration and Production

'provides leaders with the ability to understand the dynamics that relate the business to their organization, communicate this understanding, and move the organization into different directions ensuring continued success.'
Emad A. Elrafie, Ph.D., Executive Manager – Delta R

'*Managing from Clarity* should be read by all managers involved in strategic planning. It makes life easier.'
Arturo Vaca, Director of Strategic Planning, Servicios Industriales Peñoles

'*Managing from Clarity* is a strategic lens that helps reaffirm, or define, the organization's current and future direction.'
Ernesto Enei, Gerente de Geo-Informática, SAPAL
(Sistema de Agua Potable y Alcantarillado de León)

'Using the *Managing from Clarity* process has revealed some surprising interactions . . . and confirmed the value of surveillance data.'
Kate Hendricks, MD, MPH&TM, Board Certified Preventive Medicine, Texas

Acknowledgements

The main concept for this book, the Managing from Clarity process, is truly part of a continuing evolution that began over seven years ago. The driving intent behind this evolution has always been to make systems thinking tools practical and useful to decision-makers across a wide range of industries facing a host of complex situations. What we have achieved so far, we owe to the wonderful laboratory of real life provided by our clients and colleagues over the past seven years.

In addition to the authors, our team consists of Luz Maria Puente, Conrado Garcia Madrid, Annabel Membrillo Jimenez, and Leslie Ritchie-Dunham. They have been an integral part of developing, testing, and delivering the Managing from Clarity tools.

We have tested, taught, and evolved the concept with clients in the USA, Mexico, Canada, the UK, The Netherlands, Germany, Honduras, Venezuela, and Nigeria. It has been applied in the private sector to many industries, including mining, petroleum, health care, insurance, telecommunications, consumer products, electric utilities, Internet start-ups, high tech, and banking. In the public sector, it has been applied to municipal government, epidemic control, and antibiotic resistance. To all our clients and collaborators, we are indebted and thankful.

This journey would not have started without the initial and continuing support from the ITAM's Business School in Mexico City. Mark White and Javier Chavez Ruiz were key in introducing us to system dynamics, systems thinking, and the powerful work of Peter Senge. We gratefully thank Carlos Alcerreca and Monica Sacristan who, on behalf of the ITAM, have continued to provide us with a powerful avenue to test our newest ideas in an academic setting. We also thank the many participants in our courses over the years whose penetrating questions have led us to deeper insights.

Dr Javier Rosado's invitation to work with the Advisory Board to the Mexican Secretariat of Health was critical in developing the first building blocks in our process. We also appreciate the great support and feedback during this project that came from Dr Jorge Mendez and Dr Federico Ortiz Quesada. The case study for this project is presented throughout this book.

We thank Iran Echavarry for helping us integrate scenario planning into our work. We thank Andreas Koch for his critical evaluation and assessment of each new piece as it was brought into the process. We also thank Anne Deering, Claude Ricks, Celine Bak, Brent Snell, and Michael Puleo in our work with A.T. Kearney's Center of Excellence in London. A special thanks to Guillermo Babatz of Grupo Bal for his unflinching faith in us, participation with us, and guidance for us in the application of this idea. To Francis Gouillart, Barbara Theurkauf, and, especially, Hans Peter von Sicard of Emergence Consulting, LLC, thank you for your remarkable ability to synthesize and help us develop our process in the strategic planning arena.

Our strategic partnership with Barry Richmond and his team at High Performance Systems has constantly reminded us of the importance of keeping it simple. We owe special thanks to Phil Odence.

Scott Spann's vast experience in executive coaching has greatly influenced our thinking about how the process and tools help leaders manage from clarity. His personal commitment always reminds us that our most worthwhile work comes from our heart.

In the preparation of the manuscript, we would like to thank colleagues and friends who read many chapters, various times, providing valuable feedback on the content and its clarity. Our colleagues Luz Maria, Annabel, Conrado, and Leslie read through many versions of the text and created many of the figures and tables. Luz Maria and Annabel valiantly prepared the index, in all of its laborious glory. Academic colleagues from the University of Texas at Austin include

Jim Dyer, Ed Anderson, and Tim Ruefli, and Nikko Georgantzas from Fordham University. Colleagues in strategy consultancies include Andreas Koch at LEK/Alcar, Jorge Rufat-Latre at Strategos, Usman Ghani at McKinsey & Company, Kristin Cobble and Scott Spann at Generative Strategies. Friends and family include C. Jay Forrest, Cleon Dunham, Jane Dunham, Beth Greenfield, Pat Rind, and Skit Rabbino. Antonio Sacristan, former Director of Strategic Planning for Pemex, provided insight into the value and potential limitations for the approach presented in the book. The text is better for their help. Any remaining mistakes are ours.

We would like to thank our Publishing Editor, Diane Taylor, and Editorial Assistant Anne Flynn, our Production Editor Viv Wickham, and Peter Hudson in Marketing at John Wiley & Sons for their support during the project.

We would like to thank our parents. Cleon and Jane Dunham have provided undivided support over many years, manifest in as many ways as it is humanly possible to support one's children. For Jim, they are his parents, advisors, and close friends. For Hal, Skit and Mitchell Rabbino have provided unwavering support, regular guidance and basic trust. To Charles and Sherry Lewis who are a constant reminder of how to live life fully, passionately, and do it everyday.

Finally, we would like to give a special thanks to Leslie Ritchie-Dunham for providing the environment in which many of the initial ideas were developed. Her skill at integration and her incisive questions have made the process a much richer one.

Introduction: Why Manage from Clarity? What Does It Mean?   1

CALL FOR ACTION

Providing clarity is the essence of leadership. In an often turbulent world, leaders need tools to help them achieve this clarity. Managing from Clarity focuses leaders' attention on three key abilities: understanding the organizations they lead, communicating that understanding to their internal and external stakeholders, and knowing where, how, and when to move the organization in the desired direction. This is the leader's job and the heart of strategy, whether at the helm of a Fortune 500 firm, a multinational non-profit, a public agency, or a family-run store.

Until recently, strategy taught leaders to divide the organization into specialized disciplines with clear, optimized incentives. Leaders worried about efficiency and effectiveness within the boundaries of the organization. At a higher level, within an industry, strategic resources used to be tangible, relatively easy to purchase, and easy to build up. Now systems extend beyond the organization into dynamic industries for which the boundaries are blurring. More than ever, key internal strategic resources are inextricably linked to each other and to the outside world. Successful leaders must develop management teams with capabilities that span across functions, organizations, and industries. This added dynamic complexity challenges assumed synergies and provokes unintended consequences, which continually threaten expected performance.

To address these pressing issues, current leading research focuses on the resource-based view and systems thinking perspectives to organizational design, providing frameworks for thinking through how strategic resources interrelate and the consequences of actions taken throughout the organization over time. Now, more than ever, management's ability to understand resource dynamics, organizational design, and incentive structures, and their ability to align these with a clear corporate purpose, will determine the winners and losers of tomorrow.

Most tools and approaches used in strategic management today were developed to work in stable environments. New tools are needed to capture the impacts of today's fast-paced, complex environment on management. A new approach is needed to help guide management through this challenging environment. The goal of this book is to present leaders with a new approach and appropriate tools to help them thrive in uncertain, and dynamically complex environments.

The authors have developed and road-tested a methodology over the past seven years with a wide variety of private and public-sector clients, both large and small.[1] In the evolution of this methodology, the goal has been to provide leaders with rigorous, intuitive tools that help them lead their organizations with increased clarity. The methodology focuses on one central concept: Managing from Clarity. As we mentioned earlier, 'clarity' focuses on the leader's understanding of the system, and 'managing' focuses on two key leadership abilities: (1) the ability to communicate the leader's understanding; and (2) the ability to move the organization in the desired direction, over time.

This chapter briefly introduces the building blocks of the Managing from Clarity methodology, providing more detail about the framework and language.

THE BASIC BUILDING BLOCKS

We now focus on the three major building blocks underpinning the Managing from Clarity methodology: theory of the firm, resource-based view, and systems thinking. Then we will see how these building blocks apply to the Managing from Clarity methodology.

Theory of the firm

The 'theory of the firm' provides the foundation for all organizational issues because it asks why a particular firm exists (its purpose).[2] In its most basic form, a firm exists to achieve a globally rational objective, one far-reaching, all-encompassing goal. A Mexican conglomerate focuses on maximizing the potential for value creation over time. The Texas Department of Health Antibiotic Resistance team strives to minimize morbidity due to antibiotic resistance. The Town of Vail wants Vail to remain a premier resort and mountain community. Additionally, as depicted in Figure 1.1, firms compete with other firms for consumers and shareholders. This is the macro view.

However, firms do not do the actual work; individuals do. Individuals, in organizations of every size and shape, work hard every day to achieve their goals. Individuals have several rationales that motivate

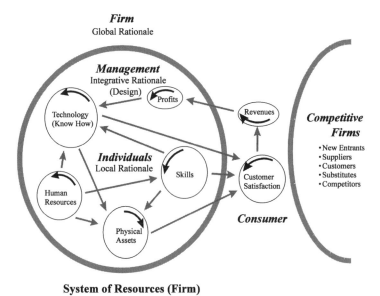

System of Resources (Firm)

Figure 1.1 Theory of the firm.

their behavior. They have personal goals (i.e., family time and quality of life) and professional goals (i.e., salary, recognition and advancement) that they manage. These goals are short term and long term. At the local level, they do their job (i.e., assembling engines, selling books, cleaning ski lifts) using multiple resources (i.e., know-how, physical assets, skills). This is the micro view.

Management's job is to integrate and coordinate the local rationale of the individuals in order to obtain the globally rational goal of the firm. Management does this by designing the structures and incentives within which individuals work, aspiring to generate and use the firm's resources in the most efficient manner over time. The resources found within the organization affect each other. This is the focus of the resource-based view.

Resource-based view

The resource-based view is a framework that provides the key jumping point from thinking about abstract, fuzzy issues, such as supplier relationship, leadership talent, or quality of client interaction, to thinking about the strategic management of the key resources that determine an organization's ability to achieve the desired overall results.[3] According to this framework, an organization is endowed with 'resources,' which are the assets that it accesses to achieve its goals. These assets include both tradable and non-tradable resources. Tradable resources include assets bought on the open market, such as land, equipment, and employees. Non-tradable resources are assets that generally cannot be purchased, such as know-how, and reputation.

The resource-based view argues for shifting from a static resource perspective to a dynamic resource perspective. This shifts management's perspective from an assumption that resources exist in a stable, predictable environment to an emphasis on the rate at which the firm's resources accumulate and are utilized or decay, over time.[4] Accumulating and maintaining resources requires thinking of resources as dynamic: these resources ebb and flow over time. This focuses attention on exploring how much and when to invest, how to maintain, and when to retire these resources.

From the resource-based view, key concerns for management include the prioritization and location of resources within the organization, which focuses on determining which resources and bundles of resources provide competitive advantage or, in other words, are strategic. Typical 'strategic resources' may include customer loyalty, production experience, and technological leads.[5] Some resources are strategic because they are shared by different groups within the firm. In many cases, the authors have observed that each group wants something different to happen to strategic resources. This occurs because these groups have different goals and rewards for management of the same resource, and thus their incentives for managing the resource push them to actions that seem logical locally, yet globally may frustrate the efforts of other groups. This interaction of resources is the focus of systems thinking, which we introduce now.

Systems thinking

> As far as preparing to work in the future, I'll tell you what I tell my children: At the personal level, you develop three basic skills: learning, critical thinking, and systems thinking. Critical thinking means you ask the right questions; systems thinking means you see the big picture. If you do that, you will have a set of skills that transcends any particular set of technical skills, which may or may not become obsolete.
>
> (Michael Hammer, co-author of *Reengineering the Corporation*)[6]

Systems thinking is about seeing, understanding, and working with 'the whole.' It focuses more on the relationships that link the parts of the whole than on the parts themselves. Systems thinking facilitates the understanding of the unintended consequences due to dynamic complexity.[7] The focus here is on 'unintended consequences' because the intuitive, seemingly rational solutions put into practice within dynamically complex systems usually create unintended consequences that leaders find difficult to comprehend.[8]

To place systems thinking in the context of general management, in 1938 Chester Barnard, previously president of New Jersey Bell Telephone, proposed two measures for how well leaders leverage the systems they manage: effectiveness and efficiency.[9] He defined *effectiveness* as the achievement of a specific desired end – this definition is not surprising. He defined an *efficient* action, however, as one where the unintended consequences of the action are less important than the attainment of the desired end – this is a radical departure from typical definitions of efficiency. Barnard's thesis can then be restated as: effective and efficient policies, derived from a systems thinking perspective, provide high leverage in systems.

As mentioned above, every system has a purpose, a reason for being. The human body works hard to keep itself alive. The automobile exists to convert energy into motion ... with us safely on board! A dump truck and a racecar are both automobiles, yet each is designed for a different purpose. An essential structure for the dump truck, such as a hydraulic lift, would completely hinder the racecar's ability to perform. The message here is that, in all systems, what drives performance is the structure, not just our desire to achieve the goal. Systems thinking provides a language to talk consistently about structures that drive performance within the organization.

To discuss and understand systems of interrelated parts requires understanding the basic concept of cause–effect linkages.[10] All actions are caused by something. Organizations mandate that managers understand those causes.[11]

Cause–effect linkages

System Dynamics is a well-developed and tested systems thinking methodology and language.[12] Causal mapping, one of the basic tools of system dynamics that will be explained in more detail in the following chapters, establishes the cause–effect relationships among the key elements, or actors, in the system being studied, and validates the internal logic of these connections. Why is it so important to document and validate these relationships? This question might be answered by looking at the value it provides.

How valuable would it be to the leadership team to share a common understanding of the business drivers of organization performance over time? To understand how each area affects each other? Usually, when discussing strategy at most organizations, the tendency is to view the different areas within the organization operating like pistons in an engine. All parts move in perfect synchronicity, each performing predictably in a stable setting. When asked about the reality of business, however, most executives observe that the different 'pistons' seem to change size and pace with each turn of the crank!

Within organizations, the knowledge of these separate elements usually resides within the heads of the area experts in different parts of the organization. Would it be helpful if there were a single platform where all strategic discussions could take place? This requires integrating disparate parts of the system into a single model or understanding of the system. Causal mapping provides a language and a method for merging and clarifying the understandings of individual experts into a single model. 'Causal maps' show the cause–effect linkages between two actions, integrating the decision goals and control information about actions with the corresponding actions.

Feedback and delays

Reductionist thinking emphasizes linear logic, such as *Product Innovation causes Sales, which causes Production, which causes Income.* To this logic, systems thinking adds feedback relationships, such as *Sales of existing products* cause *Production*, which causes *Income*, which promotes more *Sales. Income* also affects *Innovation*, which also affects *Sales of new products* (see Figure 1.2).[13] Systems thinking also introduces the effects of time delays. For example, it may take time for *Innovation* to actually affect *Sales* whereas *Income* will drive *Sales* more quickly.[14] Feedback loops and time delays drastically alter the behavior of systems and challenge traditional analysis and solutions, many examples of which will be given throughout this book.

Systems thinking provides a framework for thinking about organizations as groups of interrelated people, actions and resources. The language of systems thinking has proven beneficial in three aspects

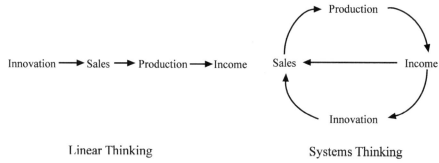

Linear Thinking   Systems Thinking

Figure 1.2 Systems thinking logic.

of managerial decision-making:

- comprehending complex systems
- sharing observations and experiences related to complex systems
- thinking about, understanding, and testing the dynamic behavior of the systems.

The rest of this chapter provides an overview of the Managing from Clarity methodology, using the three major building blocks introduced above: theory of the firm, resource-based view of strategic resources and systems thinking.

THE MANAGING FROM CLARITY METHODOLOGY

An overview

Figure 1.3 is an overview of the Managing from Clarity methodology. Starting with the building of the GRASP Map, the process flows through to the development of the Learning Interfaces. The rest of the chapter walks through this process, highlighting its purpose, main tools, typical insights, and example applications.

The first step: building the GRASP Map

The first step of the Managing from Clarity methodology, the GRASP Map and Analysis, accelerates an emerging trend in the fields of system

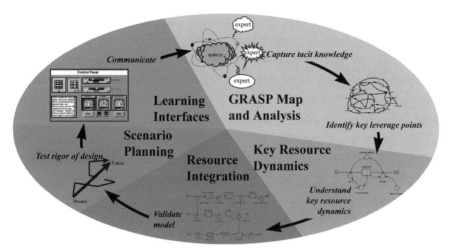

Figure 1.3 Overview of the Managing from Clarity methodology.

dynamics and systems thinking that first creates a map of the organization's overall goals, resources, actions, structure, and people and then describes these cause–effect linkages quantitatively. In order to capture tacit knowledge from the leadership team and identify key leverage points for moving the organization in the desired direction, the Managing from Clarity methodology structures the building of the first cause–effect map integrating the following five areas:

Goals focus on why the system exists.
Resources focus on the resources needed to achieve the goals.
Actions focus on how to most leverage these resources.
Structure focuses on how the resources and actions interrelate.
People focuses on how to bring the system to life.

This is the heart of GRASP. Whom do we include in the strategy process? How do we incorporate their multiple perspectives? How do we identify the strongest points of leverage in the strategy? How do we get everyone to agree on them? Strategists face these critical process questions, because they know that successful implementation of any strategy depends on getting people in the organization to both understand and identify with the strategy.

The GRASP Map and Analysis captures, integrates, and analyzes the mental models of the people that best understand how the organization works to achieve its goals. Linking the theory of the firm, resource-based view, and systems thinking foundations, the rest of this section describes how the methodology analyzes this strategic road map from the global, local, and integrative perspectives.

The framework used to identify and analyze leverage within the GRASP Map is based on understanding the three distinct perspectives in each organization, as we saw in the theory of the firm: global, local, and integrative. The global perspective represents the 'owners' of the system – the people responsible for the overall or global behavior of the system and for providing corporate resources. The local perspective represents the 'participants' in the system – the people responsible at the tactical or local level for using local and corporate resources to get things done. The integrative perspective represents the 'management' of the system – the people responsible for designing structures for and ensuring that the local level activities achieve the global goals.

Well-planned actions within different parts of the organization, however, often conflict with each other and with the overarching stakeholder goal, usually some form of value maximization. The Managing from Clarity methodology helps leaders understand how to better structure their interrelated policies that link different areas of the firm. Managing from Clarity tools integrate all of the organizational parts into a single model, making the following explicit to managers:

1   What the system's overarching purpose is?
2   How does the system-wide structure want to behave globally?
3   How does the 'local' structure want to behave?
4   How does system-wide and local rationale affect each other?

The Managing from Clarity methodology sheds light on the understanding of and potential leverage within each of these perspectives, making them explicit and open for dialog and subsequent action.

Global perspective

The initial step in the GRASP Map and Analysis phase is to create a dynamic resource map of the system. Having done that, we begin an analysis of the system in greater depth. The globally rational perspective facilitates understanding of the highest level of expectations for the behavior of the system – what the 'owners' of the system expect. This perspective provides insight into the feasibility and implications of the desired behavior at the global level.

Briefly, the global perspective phase uses three tools: Global Goals, archetypes, and Feedback Structure Behavior Analysis. The Global Goal Analysis determines why the system exists, how that goal is achieved, and how it has behaved over time. Archetype Analysis shows how the system will tend to continue to behave over time. The Feedback Structure Behavior Analysis provides initial quantitative understanding into how key policies affect behavior within the system.

Typical insights in this phase derive from making the organization's global goal explicit, and developing a shared understanding of how each subsystem affects that goal. Though most leadership teams think that their global goal is clear to all, our experience shows that there is often lack of agreement within the team and between the team and their direct reports.

Within leadership teams, all members have different mental models of the world, to the point where they often view the purpose of the same organization differently, and most leaders that we have worked with believe that of the knowledge they have of the systems, their direct reports have at most 50% of that clarity. So, how can an organization work towards the same goal, if they do not even share a common understanding of the global goal? Making explicit the global goal and sharing that understanding go a long way towards fixing this issue.

For example, a member of the executive portfolio management team of a large utility entering a highly competitive, deregulated market started the exercise by stating that obviously the team's goal was to maximize earnings before interest and taxes (EBIT). As senior management had been reinforcing this concept recently, many other members shook their heads in the affirmative, until someone clarified that they really were maximizing shareholder value. Another asked if that was actually total returns to shareholders. Then another added, almost jokingly, that this was true, given the constraint of keeping regulators happy. Someone else then, getting more serious, suggested that they also had to keep internal customers happy, to maximize the benefit of the portfolio. As you can see, this simple yet valuable exercise showed that there were multiple points of view and that the solution was not so obvious. On the other hand, the group quickly came to a consensus that they existed to create value for stakeholders and which groups should be included.

Local perspective

The local perspective looks at each of the subsystems and the drivers of the behavior they exhibit. This perspective provides insight into the implications and consistency of the desired behavior for each group within the system.

The local perspective phase presents two tools: the Systemic Stakeholders' View and the Trend Analysis. The Systemic Stakeholder's View highlights the strategic resources shared by different groups or subsystems, and the conflict created by that shared use as each group or subsystem has different incentives in how to use and develop the shared resource. The Trend Analysis makes explicit how individuals within the local groups view the resources for which they are responsible, and their expectations for the behavior of those resources over time.

Typical insights from this perspective come from making explicit for the first time our expectations for certain resources and how they are interrelated, checking the consistency of these expectations, and from seeing how our expectations about other groups differ within the organization. Groups often hear from their colleagues, for the first time, how other areas of the business actually work, how they are managed, and why.

For example, to do this exercise the management team of an industrial equipment manufacturer divided into its four different functional areas. Each area wrote down how the different resources within their area had behaved in the past and how they expected them to behave in the future. They did the same exercise for the other three groups. The exercise seemed obvious and straightforward to them, until the results were consolidated. The teams were shocked to find that they had been very wrong about the other groups, and even worse that the other groups had been completely wrong about their own area! This highlighted the lack of understanding about crucial resources the groups shared and why the groups acted the way they did. By then using the GRASP map to tell their own story, all groups were able to finally understand what each group did and why.

Comparing the global and the local perspectives assesses the 'current state' of the system. These two perspectives have focused the team's attention on why the system exists, the resources and actions that are in place to achieve the global goal, how the whole system is structured, and how people's rationales affect the system's behavior. This provides a view of the current state of the system. This assessment highlights and makes explicit the potential gaps between the owners' desires and what the system is structured to deliver.

Having completed both the global and local level analyses, one can compare the vision that the two perspectives provide. The global and local perspectives often provide shockingly different views of the same system. On the one hand, the global perspective indicates that Stakeholder Subgoals primarily exist within reinforcing feedback loops (i.e., the business growth cycle), where the explicit purpose of the organization is to create continuously increasing value for the system's 'owners.' On the other hand, the local perspective indicates that management of most of the internal resources (i.e., assembly capacity) primarily exists within balancing feedback loops, with the explicit purpose of utilizing these resources as efficiently as possible. This paradox of a system where the global goal focuses on growth and the local goals focus on stability is what we call the 'Global to Local Paradox.' This paradox often creates misalignment between the strategic message that senior management proclaims and the ability of the organization to deliver.

Integrative perspective

The integrative perspective provides four tools to assist leaders integrate the local potential of the individuals in the organization to achieve the global goals: MICMAC Analysis, Stakeholder Relationship Assessment, Performance Measurement, and Structural Changes. MICMAC analysis shows the relative influence of each resource on the movement of other resources in the system, as well as the relative exposure to the other resources captured in the GRASP map. This analysis highlights the interconnectivity of strategic resources and begins to prioritize the level of management that should design policies and monitor the strategic resources. The Stakeholder Relationship Assessment describes how each of the major players in the organizations views its relationship with the other players. This highlights potential conflicts arising from different perspectives, as well as explicitly prioritizing the relationships on which each group will focus.

The Performance Measurement Analysis makes explicit the existing performance expectations for each group in the organization, how that feeds the current overall behavior of the organization, what potential performance indicators could be to promote an integrated approach towards achieving the organization's global goal, the associated core competencies, and the type of culture those new indicators represent. The Structural Change Analysis examines how changes in information and material flows in the organization, the policies that regulate those flows, and how changes in time delays all affect the overall behavior of the organization.

Pulled together, these analyses inform each other. For example, understanding how resources in one group affect resources in another group affects how those groups prioritize their relationship, which affects the performance indicators they use to measure the success of that relationship. Typical insights from the integrative perspective focus on how the current design of the organization, including how the incentives for each group affect each other, and how those incentives are communicated, often creates many of the difficulties that the leadership team had attributed to external causes.

For example, in a high-tech start-up, very clear incentives had been designed into the marketing, product development, and operations groups. Sell as much as you can. Develop the best product possible. Maximize operational efficiency. This set of incentives did not reflect an organization focused on having the best product a customer could want, but rather the product they could develop the best for the lowest cost. This shocked the leadership team. They believed that they were a customer-driven developer. By working through the shared strategic resources, the inter-group relationships and influences, the team developed a set of incentives that would promote the groups working together to understand the customer and deliver an excellent product to those expectations.

Most organizational structures evolve without much thought to design.[15] Solely based on having combined synergistic resources, the firm creates a competitive advantage, almost unconsciously. Though this is often very good news, management often cannot explain the success of this combination. This poses the significant challenge of re-creating the same synergistic effect as the corporate structure changes over time, through acquisition, sale, reorganization, or changing conditions. Vail's premier setting has provided it with a strong competitive advantage, until the recent onslaught of premier alternatives, like access to international resorts and cruises. A monopoly in electric utility provision protected a very successful firm from competitive forces for years. Very successful computer manufacturers grew up as hardware companies, then found themselves receiving more revenues from servicing the installed base than from selling hardware.

The Managing from Clarity framework enriches this need for corporate design. Corporate design focuses on deliberately identifying and exploiting, and in many cases creating, the leverage hidden in the formal and informal corporate structure – consciously choosing structures and incentives that leverage management's ability to provide sustainable competitive advantage.

As corporate designers, management can leverage the firm's resources at three levels of the system structure: (1) the actions of

individuals; (2) the goals that drive individual actions; and (3) alignment of the goals of multiple individuals across the organization.

Working with a variety of clients – well meaning, intelligent, successful clients – we continue to find well-planned actions, within
different parts of the organization, repeatedly conflicting with each
other and with the overarching, stakeholder-value maximization
goal. Managing from Clarity helps managers structure their interrelated policies and generate effective leverage for value creation
over time. This is crucial because management's ability to unravel
the mysteries of their complex, dynamic decision-making environment
will profoundly affect strategic actions and future firm performance.

Having completed the GRASP Map and Analysis step, now what?
Since the intent is always to increase the decision-maker's clarity,
where to go next depends on the issues being addressed. Two of the
strongest and more common paths include moving into key resource
dynamics or scenario planning.

Moving to key resource dynamics leverages what the modeling
group has agreed are the probable issues and key resources, and
begins to take a quantified look at what actually happens dynamically
around the strategic resources and what effort is required to accumulate and maintain them. Moving to scenario planning the GRASP Map
provides an agreed-upon platform that manages the complexity of the
dialog around the impacts of the different scenarios on the organization and its ability to act. We discuss each of these steps below. Alternatively, many organizations have found the insight gained from this
step alone to be sufficient to move the organization forward – again, it
all depends.

The second step: quantifying key resource dynamics

How do we build up, maintain, and utilize the resources we have
determined to be critical to our strategy? Which actions provide the
most leverage in developing these resources? As strategists tackle
these issues, they puzzle over the complexities of managing strategic
resources over time.

The Key Resource Dynamics step of the Managing from Clarity methodology explores the counterintuitive behavior that often results from the dynamics that affect each strategic resource. This step quantifies the qualitative GRASP Map, and explores the unintended consequences of policies that affect these resources, avoiding the 'free lunch' pitfall. The Key Resource Dynamics phase also highlights the stability of the resource utilization policies, and permits quantitative testing of the recommended strategies, basically hypotheses, for accumulating, maintaining and utilizing these strategic resources over time.

While mainstream practice rightly suggests very rigorous, data-intensive validation of the model, this step follows emerging practices that focus on helping the decision-maker quickly understand the complex resource dynamics, focusing on the *net effect* required to leverage the strategic resource, and to test the decision-maker's underlying theories about resource development, maintenance and utilization.

Key Resource Dynamics pulls from the rigorous stock-flow modeling of system dynamics, and the analysis of complexity theory to provide managers with a rich understanding of what effects their strategic resources, and how these resources behave over time, under different policies. The focus, however, is on providing tools that organizational leaders can use without having advanced studies in mathematics or simulation.

Typical insights focus on the net effect of the different policies influencing strategic resources. It seems that often people think about increasing a resource by increasing the flow into it, and decreasing a resource by decreasing the flow out of it. Counter-intuitive logic, however, also shows that by decreasing (increasing) a flow into (out of) a resource more than the flow out (in), you decrease the resource over time. The same logic applies for the outflows. What results is an understanding that to increase (decrease) a resource requires that the net effect of the multiple inflows and outflows be positive (negative). Though this might seem obvious now, when applied to an organization's strategic resources, this insight is often shocking.

For example, the management team of a large health care diagnostic tool manufacturer had experienced exponential growth in its customer base over the first seven years, with growth slowing down in the past two years. This slowdown was frustrating management. Since historically all marketing efforts had been toward new users of their tools, management had increased investments in marketing, but to no avail.

During this exercise, a member of the management team noticed that if the net effect was positive, but less and less each year, then that meant that the outflows were catching up to the inflows. Nevertheless, what were the outflows to the customer base? Though they knew how many customers went to the competition, they had never studied how many customers had altogether stopped using the tools, an outflow representing almost 15% of the customer base! The results suggested that they should focus their marketing efforts on both getting new customers AND retaining exiting customers. Though this may seem very obvious now, we have regularly seen in many firms that base rate growth is more often associated with adding more than with losing less.

From this step, the most common path is to integrate the multiple strategic resources into one linked simulation of the enterprise, to determine how their interrelationships influence the organization's ability to sustainably accumulate and maintain these key resources when faced with one or more clear strategic challenges.

The third step: integrating and validating the map

Will investment in certain resources deteriorate our ability to grow other strategic resources? Given limited resources, when should we invest in the different resources and for how long, to have them all strong when we need them? Strategists confront these issues when deciding how and when to implement multiple initiatives of the corporate strategy, knowing that there are complex dynamics affecting the development of strategic resources.

The Resource Integration step of the Managing from Clarity methodology quantifies the connection among the key resources explored in the prior step of the methodology, permitting the integrated testing of the multi-pronged intervention strategies.

While mainstream practice suggests high-resolution models that provide specific answers (read: the predicted number), in the Managing from Clarity methodology, this step follows emerging trends that focus on keeping the map simple and insightful, accurately reflecting the expert mental model shared by the leadership team in its decision-making process. In this process, the focus is on shared understanding of dynamic behavior and not on data fitting. Nonetheless, in populating even these high-level models with key data, many assumptions about 'how long,' 'how much,' and 'whom it affects' often surprise the management team.

This step provides Resource Integration, Model Validation, Leverage Point Identification, and Dynamic Hypothesis Testing. Resource Integration pulls from the GRASP map logic to explore potential relationships between the key resources in the model. Model Validation uses traditional sensitivity analysis as well as other analyses from the GRASP Map and Analysis step to determine those actions that most leverage the system's ability to achieve its global goal. Dynamic Hypothesis Testing formulates the hypotheses and then tests them in this mathematical simulation environment.

This step typically provides two important insights into the behavior of complex systems. First, the adage 'local optimization leads to global sub-optimization' comes to life when actions that maximize local resources have strong negative impacts on resources in other areas. Second, the points of highest leverage in a system are often most difficult to find, given that they often are linked indirectly to variables of most interest.

For example, a deregulated telecommunications firm placed strong incentives on innovative technologies, as the customer perceived added functionality as a strength. Strong innovation in technology, however, made obsolete the skill base of the call center staff providing customer service – the service representatives could not keep up with the ever-changing technology. Call centers were being asked to respond to services they had heard about, but had no idea how they worked. How often does management look to save a budget by cutting training and or hiring to push harder on gaining share by promoting new product development and launches? The more insightful question is knowing *how much* and *when* to cut or add resources.

From this step, there are two common paths, including scenario planning, and learning interface development. Moving to scenario planning, the team uses the integrated model to test the impact of different assumptions about the future on the organization's viability. Moving to learning interfaces, the team develops an interface that maximizes the ability of a wider audience to learn the lessons of the exercise, or 'fly' the organization to share in the issues, challenges, and decisions facing management.

The fourth step: scenario planning and strategic foresight

Are the strategy and the structure we have designed the strongest for the unknown future? What are some of the key assumptions that we have about the future that might affect the strategy and structure we choose? Strategists by definition are forward-looking, needing to explore the rigor of their design against numerous plausible futures that may unfold.

The Scenario Planning and Strategic Foresight step investigates critical concerns across this range of possible futures, as well as the organization's potential ability to survive and thrive in such environments. This step tests the rigor of the organization's underlying assumptions and policies, which were made explicit in the GRASP Map and analysis, Key Resource Dynamics and Resource Integration steps. The focus during this step is on policies that promote sustainable, systemic balance and leverage of the organization's efforts.

While mainstream practice suggests using simulation models to run sensitivity analyses, this step follows the emergent field of scenario planning and strategic foresight, focusing on understanding future trends that might have significant impact on the organization, and severe testing of the shared understanding implicit in the map and previous analyses.

This step provides tools for integrating strategic foresight and scenario planning into the modeling process. From this step, leadership teams typically discover insights into emerging trends that might have significant impact on the rigor of the organization's policies in the future, as well as making explicit different underlying assumptions about key dimensions in the future.

For example, a national oil company began its strategic planning exercise by presenting the plans from each department. Each department painted a splendid picture of technological leadership. The scenario planning exercise then walked through the assumptions underlying the projected successes. A key assumption was that the national government would invest heavily in the oil company. Under each of the four scenarios developed, not once did the government opt to invest heavily in the level of research capacity required to be a technology leader in the oil industry. The government could not, as it had to deal with the social costs of the rapidly growing population, and the oil company was a key contributor to national income. By questioning this assumption, the leadership team was able to scale their strategic plan to one that was plausible and still helped achieve the company's overall goals.

From this step, most teams opt to either develop a learning interface to communicate the model, continue modeling to capture the new policies or embed the existing work into an on-going strategic planning process. Moving to learning interfaces integrates the rich scenarios into the story that the wider community will receive. Moving to further modeling explores the impact of new policies on the model of the organization over time. Embedding the simulation tool in the strategic planning process provides a rigorous, real-time approach to ensuring that a systemic perspective is included in the development of corporate policy.

The fifth step: learning interfaces

How do we communicate our strategy so that the people in the organization understand the strategy and feel as if they own it? Strategists face this issue of communicating and translating the strategy for the people in the organization who will implement the strategy.

The Learning Interfaces step of the Managing from Clarity methodology provides a vehicle for communicating the logic and drivers behind the desired policies to a larger audience in a highly effective, self-teaching way. This step advances the emerging trend of facilitating self-teaching and learning, to understand the key issues and dynamics. This step relies on the previous analysis to determine what key learning to highlight and which decision points and outputs should be included in the interface to support these messages. This may require modification to the existing integrated mathematical model or the development of specific models built to transmit specific messages gleaned from the prior steps of the methodology.

Three types of learning interfaces typically may be developed, depending on the type of communication desired: dashboards, learning laboratories, and learning environments. The common ingredient of the three is an interface that permits the user to interact with the quantified model easily, simulating different policies in an accelerated fashion. Dashboards provide an interface between the integrated resource model and the user, permitting the user to control certain inputs and see certain outputs. Learning laboratories provide a dashboard, as well as indicating the causality of the actions and consequences. Many learning laboratories include audio-visual feedback from the model, creating the cultural environment that pressures the user to make certain decisions. Learning environments provide learning laboratory attributes, as well as interactive coaching about the results obtained and how to obtain better results in the future by explaining the underlying causality creating the problem. Clearly, the selection of which interface to develop is based on specific and different needs.

Typical insights in this step include what to teach and what not to teach, and how to facilitate others learning for themselves. These are very powerful tools for communicating strategy across the organization. For example, for a large insurance company, initial iterations of the model provided dashboards for the users most involved in the modeling process to validate the model. Later exercises used learning laboratories that integrated feedback from key constituencies to assimilate the pressure managers had to behave in suboptimal ways. The final, and more simplified version of the model used a learning environment, so that the model could be used in training as a stand-alone trainer of current organizational policies.

CASE STUDIES[16]

The Managing from Clarity methodology is cumulative, in both learning and development. We have chosen two specific cases in order to show the progression of the process and maintain the continuity of the analyses. We also include short examples throughout the book to offer insight into the range of issues and industries where this work has been applied.

To select the case studies to present in the book, we focused on two key, organization-classifying dimensions, public versus private sector and high versus low resource availability. The dengue case study represents the public sector with low resource availability. The Mint case study represents the private sector with high resource availability.

- *Dengue.* The Mexican Secretary of Health faced a potential epidemic in 1995 with scarce financial resources. As the mosquito-transmitted disease dengue crossed Guatemala towards Mexico, the worst-case estimate of fatalities reached 16 million people. Experts from around the world arrived to advise the Secretary of Health on disease transmission characteristics, pathologies and treatment, mosquito control programs, and disease detection and isolation techniques. The Secretary had to decide, with very little money and multiple expert opinions, how to minimize the impact of this potential disaster on the Mexican population.
- *Mint.*[17] The Chief Executive Officer of a prestigious European capital equipment design and assembly firm in a highly cyclical industry saw the first indications of a strong upswing in consumer demand. Board members were pushing to maintain high market

share, which resulted from their strong tradition in product design, by dedicating resources to sales efforts. The CEO had to decide when to invest in additional assembly capacity, while maintaining minimal financial risk to the firm.

These two case studies and the many examples we will provide come from our actual work over the past seven years. As with the clients in these cases, we hope that you find the framework helpful in thinking strategically about complex organizational issues. We also hope that you find the tools useful. We dedicate the rest of the book to exploring in more detail each of the steps of the Managing from Clarity methodology.

The GRASP Map: Capturing and Integrating Expert Understanding of the Business Model 2

Distinguished guests, I will summarize the learned opinions, which the many experts have presented to us in the past two hours, and what I intend to do, with a single diagram.

> (Mexican Secretary of Health's advisor to the international conference on dengue control, as he displayed the dengue QualMap on the large screen at the National Academy of Medicine)

The previous chapter introduced the resource-based view of the organization and systems thinking as the basic building blocks for the Managing from Clarity process (Clarity). Starting with this chapter, Clarity will be applied to two case studies. The next seven chapters will follow the steps of the Clarity process, giving greater insight into how to leverage complex social systems. Along the way, specialized tools will be introduced as needed.

As the process starts, the focus is on capturing and integrating expert understanding of the business model. The intent is to initiate dialog and feedback within the management team early on to maximize the amount of insight gained by the team. Early insight and team learning around an integrated business model provide the foundation to continue the rigorous work of exploring and testing the team's understanding of the dynamics that drive behavior over time in their organization. This approach helps the team gain more clarity about the most powerful policy and incentive design for the desired strategy of their organization.

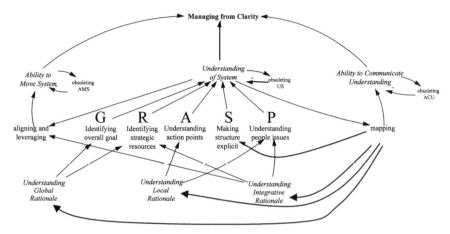

Figure 2.1 Managing From Clarity framework.

Using the language developed in Chapter 1 to understand the Managing from Clarity framework, management exists to achieve an overarching goal for the organization. The process has three focal points that guide management in reaching this goal: develop a systemic understanding of the system; use leverage to move the system; and provide an effective mechanism to communicate this understanding to the multiple stakeholders. The Clarity process is practical and practicable, because it integrates the global perspective of the system with the local perspectives, providing insight into better policy, strategy formulation, and implementation, to achieve the overarching goal (see Figure 2.1).

GRASP MAP AND ANALYSES

The first phase of the Managing from Clarity process is to build a qualitative map of the system under study called a QualMap. The purpose of the QualMap is:

1   to capture the best and most relevant knowledge of the system's resources and their interrelationships for the global strategy – to understand holistically how the system works
2   to integrate this knowledge into a single model

3   to analyze and understand how to leverage the resources in the system

4   to initiate dialog into the strategic design of policies and incentives throughout the system to best achieve the global goal.

The process starts by addressing 'the most difficult question' that challenges the group. Typically, the team wants to change the behavior of a key indicator or behavioral output of their system that is the hallmark of their strategy. With this in mind, the first step is to understand the team's goal.

GLOBAL GOAL ANALYSIS

It is crucial to clearly define the team's purpose.[1] A lackluster approach to this critical, and often difficult, piece of the process will generally doom the rest of the process.[2] The purpose centers the team on the critical concern or issue they want to answer. Guiding questions to ask the group are:

1   What specific issues keep you up at night?
2   Do the issues have intended and potentially unintended consequences that would affect the successful management of the issue, over time?
3   Are you more interested in (a) understanding how your strategic policies around the issues affect their behavior over time, or (b) knowing a specific answer at a given point in time?
4   Do the issues contain qualitative variables that are crucial to their understanding?

Chapter 1 stated that all systems have a reason for existing. This was called the globally rational goal. The identification and analysis of global goals is referred to as the Global Goals Analysis.

The Global Goal Analysis has three components:

1   goal hierarchy analysis

2   reference behavior pattern
3   goal means–ends analysis.

These three components establish a strong foundation for the remaining process by doing the following:

- making the global goal of the system explicit;
- incorporating key participants' understanding of how their efforts affect the global goal;
- developing a shared understanding of the global goal and how each subsystem affects that goal;
- creating a common platform and language for communicating the global goal of the system to other members of the system and members of other systems.

> In articulating the global goal in the work the authors did with the Texas Department of Health's Antibiotic Resistance Team, clarifying the specific words that captured the group's understanding took almost 12 hours! Though apparently trivial at the start, each participant realized that the difference in their backgrounds, though all doctors or advanced degree professionals in public health, significantly affected their underlying assumptions about the purpose of this team. Once clarified, this goal provided the rigorous backdrop for all of the subsequent model development, analysis, and group discussions.

Goal hierarchy analysis

The first step in explicitly stating the global goal of the system requires realizing that the many participants in the system have different perspectives of that global goal. Everyone may think that they understand the same goal. Many people ask, 'Isn't the goal obvious?' Research in the behavioral sciences and years of experience in the real world show that it is anything but obvious.

When working with one group exploring their global goal, the department chair told the group, 'This is ridiculous. We wrote the goal in the six-bullet-point memo that was circulated last week.' As she started to read the memo, the facilitator asked her to stop and asked everyone to write down their 'expert understanding' of the global goal of the system that they had all been working on for two years. When the facilitator read the statements from the five participants, they had five clearly different 'global goals.' It was obvious that the group did not share the same understanding of the purpose for the system in which they worked. By working through the exercise, they were able to place all their partial perspectives together into a much stronger, and now shared, understanding of their purpose, their system goal.

In determining the global goal of the system, the group needs to ask, 'What is the problem?' and 'Why does this system exist?' At this point, brainstorming or many other elicitation methods, helps establish what the group thinks the goal is.[3] This list most often reflects what each participant's highest order operational goal is. After all, it is what they do every day. With each item listed, the group continues by asking, 'Why would we want that?' This usually leads to a higher level, or more aggregated, goal. This exercise continues, interlinking and aggregating the different lower order goals until the group arrives at a single, overarching goal that resonates with the entire group. This usually means that the global goal, at the strategic level, generally corresponds to a fundamental value in the purpose of the organization.

Dengue case study

As will be seen throughout the Clarity process, knowing when to stop aggregating is crucial. There is a basic rule of thumb for determining the boundary, or when enough is enough. The factors that most strongly influence the global goal must lie within the system being modeled. For example, 'enhance the Mexican citizen's standard of living' is beyond the scope of the Mexican Secretariat of Health's Epidemiological Control group, because standard of living also includes education, income and other social factors. The factors affecting 'minimize morbidity due to dengue' lie within the sphere of

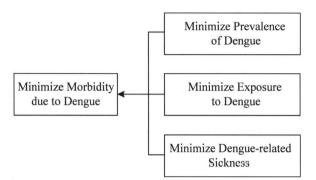

Figure 2.2 Goal hierarchy analysis for dengue case study.

influence of the Mexican Secretariat of Health's epidemiological control system. Thus when new goals fall outside the group's scope, it is time to stop and take a step back.

After defining the global goal, explore it in more detail. What is the organization going to do to achieve the global goal? The subgoals under the global goal should exhaustively describe 'what' to do to satisfy the global goal. In the case of dengue, the very real possibility of an additional strain of dengue entering Mexico through Guatemala, thereby significantly raising the risk of death by this pathogen in Chiapas, Quintana Roo, and the Yucatan regions, came to the Health Minister's attention just a couple of months before its potential entry into Mexico. Faced with the challenge of what would be the most effective countermeasures given an extremely limited budget, the global goal of this team was to minimize morbidity (people getting sick and people dying) due to dengue. When looking at 'what' needed to happen to achieve this goal, it became clear that people needed to stop from ever being exposed in the first place, they needed to be taken care of if they got sick, and the health officials needed to try to keep the sick from dying (see Figure 2.2).

Mint case study

In the Mint case study, the board was facing a difficult series of events. After years of a market downturn, demand was picking up and sales were increasing, but slightly less than the pace of market demand.

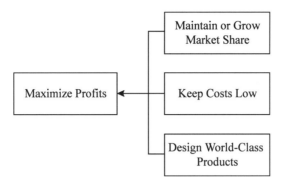

Figure 2.3 Goal hierarchy analysis for Mint case study.

Worse still, their quarterly financial reporting kept showing a degeneration of their margins as operating expenses were increasing. How was this possible, after being so successful at cost reduction over the past downturn? In order to focus on this problem, the board generated the global goal of 'maximizing profits.' Grouping their subgoals for achieving that global goal identified three common factors (see Figure 2.3), directed at the marketplace, assembly, and customers. The market-driven goal focused on maintaining or growing market share. The internal process-driven goal focused on continuation of the strong cost-reduction efforts of the past seven years. The customer factor focused on continuing to design excellent products.

Having determined the system's purpose, the next component in the Global Goal Analysis is to understand the dynamic behavior pattern of that goal over time.

Reference behavior pattern

A 'reference behavior pattern' (RBP) solidifies the group's initial and guiding dynamic hypothesis of what they believe is their global goal. A RBP is the *pattern of behavior* identified as problematic in achieving the global goal and subgoals of the system, to which the team will *refer* throughout the Managing from Clarity methodology.[4]

We highlight again the importance of including time as the underlying element of all of these analyses in the Clarity approach. By including time, the team can explicitly draw and analyze non-linear relationships more effectively. Traditional analysis of business dynamics assumes that the path from one time period to the next will be straight, whereas the systems thinking approach embraces the notion that cause–effect relationships and their behavior patterns in real life rarely move in straight lines. Therefore, it is important to choose a relevant time frame over which to measure the behavior of the global goal. Relevancy here refers to the time frame in which sufficient historical and future behavior provide a pattern, but not so long as to be irrelevant to the current strategic initiative.

The team then traces the behavior of this variable on a graph over time. The past maps historical data, and the future maps expected and desired performance. This seemingly innocent graph provides a wealth of information into the behavior seen, the preferred behavior, and the causal structure that creates these behaviors.

Dengue case study

For the dengue case study, the Mexican Secretariat of Health had repeatedly seen sudden outbreaks of mosquito-transmitted diseases in the tropical areas, as seen in Figure 2.4.[5] This RBP provided significant insight into the causal structure that would generate this behavior.

For the dengue case study, the relevant time frame included two outbreak cycles. Since the outbreaks occur annually, the team chose

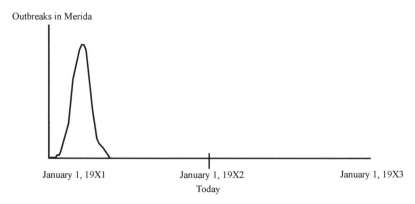

Figure 2.4 RBP for dengue case study.

to start the RBP one year in the past and extended one year into the future.

Historically, the number of outbreaks remains flat at zero for nine months of the year (see Figure 2.4). Around April, the numbers swell up very quickly to a peak and decrease as quickly, over a two- to three-month period. This indicates a system structure that is stable or balanced for most of the year and then grows and collapses exponentially for part of the year, returning to the balanced zero state. In other words, a balancing mechanism interacts with a reinforcing mechanism, with the balancing mechanism dominating most of the time and the reinforcing dominating every now and then. More examples of feedback interaction will be given later in this chapter. In the ideal future, there would never be an outbreak, that is, never a strong increase at any time during the year. Significant changes in system management will be required to achieve this radical change from the behavior of the current system.

Mint case study

For the Mint case study, management historically focused mostly on revenues. Though the market had grown rapidly, in the recent past, Mint's revenues grew slowly. Digging into this difference uncovered that they were working extra hard to maintain their market share of new orders. They interpreted the slow increase in net revenues concurrent with dramatic increases in gross sales, as decreasing revenues per engine. This led to a historical RBP focusing on net revenues per engine over time, as seen in Figure 2.5. Overlaying this with RBPs for gross revenues and costs, a very rich picture unfolds.

In the past, revenues and costs followed similar growth curves, implying close linkage and strong integration. Within the company, however, Marketing and Assembly were managed as separate functions. This organizational structure suggests an independent relationship. Worse yet, since costs outpaced revenues up to today, there was a multiplier exaggerating the cost effect, indicating a deteriorating situation from the past until 'today.' The declining cost and rising gross revenue lines indicate the desired future RBP.

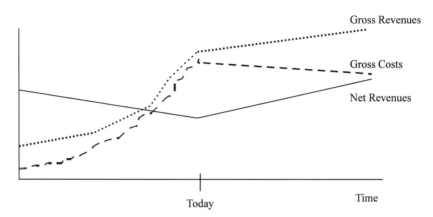

Figure 2.5 Subgoal RBP's for Mint case study.

For the Mint case study, the relevant time frame included one to two industry cycles. Since the industry cycle is about eleven years, the board chose thirty years, starting the RBP fifteen years ago and extended fifteen years into the future, allowing a full cycle in the future.

In the above case studies, the strong difference between actual and desired behavior, as well as between expected and desired behavior, indicates that to shift behavior to that desired state requires significant changes in structure (how the areas are linked) and the incentives (people do what formal *and* informal rules of the game tell them). Determining where to apply the necessary changes in a complex system tends to be quite counterintuitive. Fortunately, the RBP exercise gives useful insight into the areas of the system that will need to change to generate the desired behavior. The Managing from Clarity methodology capitalizes on this insight to focus in quickly on those policy or structural changes that should contribute to the desired behavior. These two examples demonstrate how the RBP adds a dynamic aspect to an 'understanding of the system.'

Goal means–ends analysis

After determining the global goal, and mapping its reference behavior pattern, the team identifies the means and ends objectives that relate to the actual and desired system behavior. Whereas the Goal Hierarchy Analysis focused on understanding 'what' the team wanted to achieve, the Goal Means–Ends Analysis focuses on understanding 'how' the team will achieve these goals. Ends objectives refer to those underlying reasons for an organization's existence – why the system exists. These are the values for which the system exists, the ones the system holds as most important.

To understand goals requires differentiating between the stated, or espoused, goals of the system, and the actual or 'in-use' goals of the system.[6] The global goals network analyzes the consistency of a set of interlinked system goals and subgoals.[7] In the global goals network, the lower-level goals under any higher-level goal are the answer to the question 'How can we achieve the higher-level goal?' Since the global goal of the system corresponds to the 'values' of the system, the means goals center around those resources that create value in the system for the key stakeholders, thus they are denominated as 'value-driving' resources.

To align the goals of a system requires identifying the *stated* goals and subgoals of the system, and the *actual* goals and subgoals of the system. For this exercise to provide the most insight, we recommend mapping the stated global goal means–ends network before the causal mapping and analysis. The last step in the GRASP Map and Analysis phase of the process returns to this exercise to capture the *actual* global goal means–ends network. At that point, the analysis compares the stated goal means–ends network with the actual one to determine the degree of alignment that exists.

Dengue case study

For the Secretary of Health, the global goal is to minimize morbidity due to dengue (see Figure 2.6). Means objectives refer to the cascading set of objectives that guide achievement of the global goal. Protecting the population from epidemic outbreaks of dengue is such an example. If the value for which the system exists, its global goal, is to 'minimize morbidity due to dengue,' the resources to the far right of Figure 2.6 can be thought of as the stakeholder goals or measures of the system's

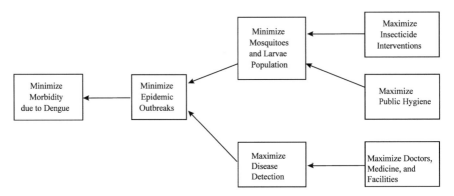

Figure 2.6 Global means–ends analysis for dengue case study.

success. Therefore, the stakeholders at this level are the mosquitoes (the root of the threat), the public (the ones directly affected by dengue) and the doctors and medical facilities (responsible for detecting and treating patients with dengue).

Mint case study

In the Mint case study, the global goal of profit maximization is achieved by maximizing revenues and minimizing costs (see Figure 2.7). If the value for which the system exists is 'maximize profits,' the 'value-driving' resources are *unit price*, *units sold* and *units produced*.

After developing the Global Goal Analysis, then the team begins to map how the stakeholder goals and their associated Value-Driving Resources, Enabling Resources, and their interrelationships

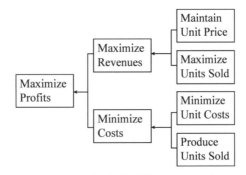

Figure 2.7 Global means–ends analysis for Mint case study.

in the system generate this behavior. The next section will introduce the basic concepts for constructing and analyzing systemic resource maps.

QUALITATIVE GRASP MAPS

The Qualitative GRASP Map (QualMap) provides a method of visually presenting a systemic understanding of the system resources.[8] This method pulls heavily from causal-loop diagram theory and application.[9] This section briefly introduces QualMaps as a basic tool for systems thinking, beginning with very simple examples to transmit key concepts. Further examples of fully integrated models are shown by the end of the chapter. This introduction will provide the reader with conversational skills for interpreting and discussing causal maps.[10]

In mapping expert mental models, QualMaps provide a rigorous method for capturing the multiple cause–effect relationships that the experts use to understand: (1) how they accumulate their desired resources; (2) the complex relationship between the resources in their part of the system; and (3) the relationship of their resources to the resources in the rest of the system. QualMaps also provide a method for integrating multiple expert mental models into a single, all-encompassing model of the system. Most importantly for the Clarity process, the QualMap is the basis for all of the remaining analyses in the GRASP Map and Analysis phase.

QualMaps use words and arrows to capture a qualitative, causal understanding of the system. A key aspect of the QualMap is that only the resources and their interrelationships are mapped, not their values. This stage focuses most on the direction of causality (will an increase in this variable cause an increase or decrease in the next variable) than with the detailed or mathematical relationship between the variables (how much will it increase or decrease). Resources use 'words' (the system's nouns). Resource inflows and out-flows use 'arrows' (the system's verbs) – thus, the term 'word-arrow diagrams.'

Pushing force   ———————————⟶ Accelerating motion

Figure 2.8 Physics example of causality.

Direct cause–effect

Let us start by mapping a simple system. Newton introduced causal thinking by stating that a *pushing force* will cause an object originally at rest to begin moving in the direction of force, and a continuing force will cause a continuing *accelerating motion*. QualMaps display this relationship as shown in Figure 2.8. This diagram reads, 'A Pushing force causes Accelerating motion.'[11]

Though the relationship shown above is definitely causal, it does not fulfill the necessary and sufficient criteria of rationality to state that:

- a pushing force always causes an accelerating motion;
- an object in an accelerating motion is determined solely by the pushing force.

The analysis is not complete because other forces are involved. One can push against a building, and it will probably not move, due to other forces. Similarly, one can hold a brick up by pushing up against it. The brick will fall when one ceases to push against it. To understand a causal influence from the systems thinking perspective, one must think about what would happen if the causal influence under examination were the only one to act on the object under study (*ceteris paribus*, that is, 'all else being the same'). If there were no frictional or structural forces restraining one from pushing the building, and one pushed it, it would move forward.

A second difficulty with causal definitions comes from the level of detail being modeled. At the individual level, it is often difficult to attribute direct causal relationships. As *safety training* increases, *accidents* decrease. This may or may not be true on an individual, or case-by-case, basis. However, leaders are generally more concerned about system behavior at an aggregate level. This claim would be confirmed by statistics showing increased safety training decreases the number of accidents per year.

To read the QualMap, the arrows connecting the words show direction of cause to effect. A negative sign (−) at the end of an arrow signifies a change in direction (read: as *costs* increase, *profits* decrease, or conversely as *costs* decrease, *profits* increase). When an arrow does not have a negative sign, the relationship is assumed to be in the same direction (read: as *revenues* increase, *profits* increase, or conversely as *revenues* decrease, *profits* decrease).

These subtle differences, which may seem to bring perplexity to causal thinking, provide the methodology with one of its key strengths − the surfacing of important assumptions and understandings held by the stakeholders about the dynamics of their system. Of even greater potential value is the examination of divergent causal opinions held by the stakeholders and experts who define these relationships within the organization. Divergence in causal opinion tends to indicate a more complex, underlying group of relationships. This exploration helps to surface key areas in the decision model. Many 'chicken and egg' relationships also show this underlying complexity indicator. Which came first, the chicken that laid the egg or the egg from which the chicken came?

As an example application, in Mint's supply chain management example *supplier productivity* affects *supplier output* (see Figure 2.9). As *supplier productivity* increases, *supplier output* increases, implying that increasing *supplier productivity* causes higher *supplier output*. *Supplier productivity* and *supplier output* (production capacity) are corporate resources; they are crucial for producing engines. *Supplier output* also

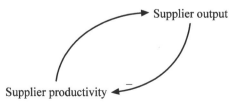

Figure 2.9 Second supply chain example of causality.

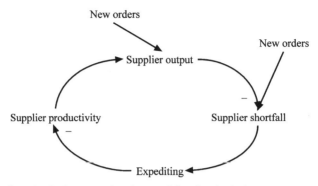

Figure 2.10 Supply chain example of causal feedback chains.

affects *supplier productivity*.[12] As *supplier output* increases significantly, machine and personnel fatigue increase and *supplier productivity* decreases. Conversely, as *supplier output* decreases due to declining demand, *supplier productivity* begins to increase.

Discussing this relatively simple relationship with the Mint's management exposed diverse opinions and surfaced the need for the team to examine this dynamic in more detail. The ensuing discussion led to a more complete QualMap of the relationship between the resources *supplier output* and *supplier productivity*. Figure 2.10 illustrates how causal relationships that are initially difficult to define can lead to new insights.[13]

If *new orders* increase, and *supplier output* remains constant, then *supplier order arrears* increases — their backlog increases. As *supplier shortfall* increases, and customers want their orders delivered, *expediting* of late orders increases. Increased *expediting* forces shifts in work priorities, decreasing *supplier labor productivity* (the number of orders each laborer can assemble per day). As *supplier labor productivity* decreases, and the *number of workers* remains the same, *supplier output* decreases. For the same level of *new orders*, and now *supplier output* decreasing, *supplier shortfall* increases even more. This creates a vicious, reinforcing downward cycle.[14]

By focusing on causal relationships in this fashion, it is possible to add a great wealth of information about how the real world works according to expert knowledge and intuition.

Qualitative variables

Interestingly, people tend to describe much of the world qualitatively, not quantitatively. These descriptions remain implicit in their understanding of how things interconnect and function over time. The variety of implicit understandings among people discussing the same issue results in differing opinions. Clarifying the qualitative aspects of these differences has been hindered by the lack of an appropriate language. Most tools only allow people to analyze the world quantitatively. The systems thinking methodology provides a simple method for mapping qualitative and quantitative resources into a QualMap, making the expert's implicit knowledge explicit and available to others in the group.

For example, adding *customer perceived delivery date* to the diagram closes the *new orders* feedback loop. As can be seen in Figure 2.11, as *supplier shortfall* increases, the *customer perceived delivery date* increases, which then causes the number of *new orders* to decrease, which eventually causes the *supplier shortfall* to decrease. The two hash marks on the arrow between *customer perceived delivery date* and *new orders* indicate that a significant delay occurs between cause and effect, between perceiving that orders are being delivered earlier or later and changing the *new orders*.

Below we summarize the steps that lead to the construction of a rigorous QualMap:

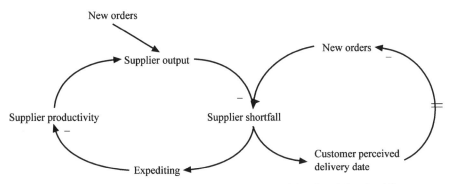

Figure 2.11 Expanded supply chain example of causal feedback for the Mint case.

1   Identify the problem.
2   Identify the key resources affecting the identified problem.
3   Determine how the key resources are interrelated, emphasizing direction of causation.
4   Analyze for redundant, indirect relationships and loops.
5   Analyze QualMap feedback structure checking for internal consistency within each loop.

QualMaps illustrate the way decisions that people make today about resources affects their ability to make decisions about those resources tomorrow. In the above example, if management were to decide to push on *new orders* without increasing the *number of workers*, then after some delay the *supplier order arrears* would begin to increase. Ultimately, this would probably frustrate the firm's ability to obtain and satisfy *new orders*.

Causal feedback loops

Causal feedback loops emphasize the process in which a cause ripples through the entire chain of causes and effects until the initial cause impacts upon itself, otherwise referred to as feedback. In the above example, there was feedback in the loop: *supplier output* created a negative change in *supplier order arrears*, which led to a change in *expediting* which influenced *supplier labor productivity* which led to decreased *supplier output*.

It is important, at this stage, to name the main function or purpose of each causal feedback loop. This begins to give an idea as to its implicit and explicit goals. For example, in Figure 2.11, the feedback loop on the right, *supplier order arrears – customer perceived delivery delay – new orders – supplier order arrears*, depicts the balancing feedback of the customer requesting fewer orders when they are delivered late. This could be titled the 'customer delay perception' balancing loop. Recording the name of the function or purpose in the middle of the loop helps record the model sections, as the model becomes larger and more interrelated, and allows us to analyze the major elements of the system, without having to reread each section each time.

By definition, two types of feedback exist – positive and negative. Positive feedback reinforces behavior creating exponential growth. Positive feedback loops are also referred to as reinforcing loops. The snowball rolling down the hill exemplifies this behavior – it gains momentum as the snowball grows larger while racing down the hill.[15] Negative feedback compensates behavior. As the snowball reaches the bottom of the hill, the friction compensates the snowball's momentum, slowing it down. Negative feedback loops are also referred to as compensating or balancing loops. The body's compensating response to a change in temperature exemplifies this behavior. If the body is too warm, it will sweat so that the evaporation of the liquid on the skin can cool the body down – the body seeks to maintain a constant corporal temperature.

QualMaps are a key tool to facilitate the understanding of the role feedback plays in dynamic decision environments. QualMaps tell the ongoing story within the system. In the dengue case, an example of a reinforcing feedback loop is shown in the *mosquito-larvae-mosquito* QualMap in Figure 2.12. As the number of *mosquitoes* increases, there is an increase in the number of *larvae* that they lay, which 're-inforces' the number of *mosquitoes* – a reinforcing cycle.

However, a basic tenet of systems thinking emphasizes that physical systems have a limit and cannot grow forever. Something will always limit growth. Periodic climate changes, such as wind and temperature changes kill a high percentage of the *mosquitoes*. As seen in Figure 2.12,

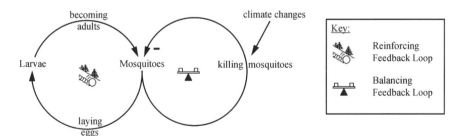

Figure 2.12 Reinforcing and balancing feedback loops.

we can see the growth cycle of mosquitoes and larvae and the balancing cycle of climatic changes limiting the mosquito population growth.

QualMaps also provide the framework for much of the analysis that will locate the leverage points in the system (e.g., which resources will provide the most leverage for achieving the system's stated goals).

Caveats to QualMaps

There are also some caveats to QualMaps. Proper interpretation of QualMaps requires that they be thought out, tested and presented rigorously, leaving little room for multiple, contradicting interpretations. If the QualMaps do not provide straightforward relationships and tell a clean, logical story, others will probably misinterpret it. This creates subsequent problems in analyzing the system. Successful systems thinking depends on rigorous QualMaps for correct interpretation. Defining the variables in concise, mutually agreed terms decreases ambiguity and increases the likelihood of a successful QualMap. On a practical note, it is highly recommended to make a glossary of the variables used in the map as it is built. At times, these variables aggregate several complex elements. This list helps maintain clarity and consistency in the use of these terms.

At a global consumer goods manufacturing site, the monthly reporting of sales resulted in three different numbers: dollar value sold, number of units sold and gross receipts including value added tax. Each had a different purpose internally and a different audience internally within the corporation. The purpose of the exercise had to be clearly understood before the correct name for 'Sales' could be articulated.

Case studies

Two fully developed high-level QualMaps are presented for the dengue (see Figure 2.13) and Mint (see Figure 2.14) case studies. As

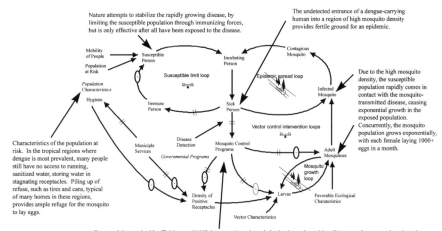

Figure 2.13 QualMap for dengue case study.

happened in these cases, a much more detailed map was developed initially to ensure that each perspective was appropriately represented. The analyses are performed using this more detailed map. In order to communicate the findings more effectively, however, it is often necessary to aggregate and simplify the QualMap into a high level

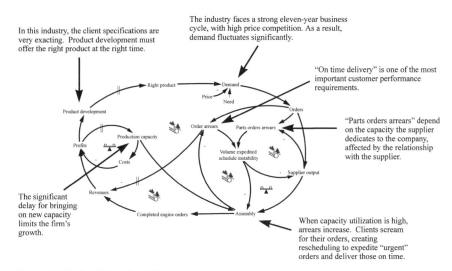

Figure 2.14 QualMap for Mint case study.

representative model. It must be detailed enough so that all relevant stories can be told with the map, but simple enough to see only the major cause–effect links. To do this, the experts within the organization were asked to help aggregate and simplify groupings of similar variables to provide the high level QualMaps seen below. To read the QualMaps, start at any point and follow the causal logic through the model. This technique of including the story along with the Qual-Map helps minimize misinterpretation, by making the story and underlying assumptions explicit. This also facilitates the ability for other groups to question and understand the key assumptions.

Tools for group dialog

These two QualMaps show how to incorporate many perspectives of the causal understanding of a system into a single model. These models have proven to be very powerful tools for handling the complexity involved in dialog about systems. The models create excellent guides for group dialog, as all the relevant logic understood by the team about the issue being modeled is explicit in the model.[16]

In one exercise, we were looking at the key elements to develop a customer-oriented strategy, recently subject to incoming competitors. As the work progressed, a clear picture was drawn around the customer experience and the internal competition management had structured between Internet Services and Customer Services in the market. With deeper analysis, the group was able to see that having the training to address new authors on the company website was the key lever splitting these two groups apart, a strategic variable way off either group's business radar.

A very important characteristic of the QualMap development centers on group facilitation of the exercise. Far from trivial, this aspect often determines or limits the successful capture, analysis and communication of the QualMap.[17]

QualMap summary

This section highlighted the construction of QualMaps – cause–effect chains linked in closed-loop feedback structures that may behave non-linearly over time. QualMaps focus attention on (1) the actors in the system, (2) the local and corporate resources they use to achieve their local goals, and (3) how they all interrelate to generate system-wide behavior.

CHAPTER LEARNING SUMMARY

This chapter addressed the first step in the Clarity process, building the QualMap to gain a better understanding of the system. This is one of the main concerns in the Managing from Clarity process. The global goal of the system was defined, its behavior over time described, the key drivers of that behavior examined, and the interrelationships in the system mapped. Within the GRASP Map and Analysis phase, this chapter accomplished the first two objectives of capturing and integrating knowledge of the interrelated system resources into a single map, using QualMaps. Now Chapter 3 will begin the QualMap analysis.

The Top to Bottom Gap: **3**
Making Explicit the Global
and Local Perspectives of the
System

Being experts in the area, I thought we all knew what the terms we shared meant and, of course, we all agreed on them. We didn't! The Managing from Clarity process systematically identified the key concepts to discuss and the framework within which to dialog about how we each understood different perspectives within the system. Probably one of the stronger team building exercises we've ever done.

(A senior staff engineer at Royal Dutch/Shell)

GRASP – GLOBAL AND LOCAL PERSPECTIVES

The framework used to identify and analyze leverage within the Qual-Map is based on understanding that there are essentially three distinct perspectives in each system: global, local and integrative. As shown in Chapter 1, the global perspective represents the 'owners' of the system – the people responsible for the overall or global behavior of the system and for providing corporate resources. The local perspective is represented by the 'participants' in the system – the people responsible at the tactical or local level for using local and corporate resources to get things done. The integrative perspective is represented by the 'management' of the system – the people responsible for designing structures for and ensuring that the local level activities achieve the global goals.

Let's introduce two terms we will use in this chapter. All organizations are built on two major types of resources, Value Driving and

Enabling Resources. Value Driving Resources (VDR) allow the organization to achieve its overarching goal. Enabling Resources (ER) are resources that are accumulated and utilized over time to build up the VDRs. At a high level, the VDRs indicate *what* the organization must do, and the ERs reflect *how* this will be done over time.

In terms of the Managing from Clarity process, we have progressed from the identification of the key causal relationships, as built in the QualMap, and now venture into the deeper analysis of these relationships and their role in the organization. The GRASP framework is the link between performing the analysis and developing concrete actions for management (see Figure 3.1).

In this next step of the Managing from Clarity process, we will analyze the QualMap, uncovering embedded assumptions about these relationships and generating insights regarding:

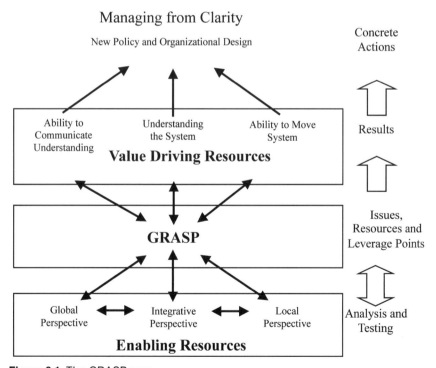

Figure 3.1 The GRASP map.

- how the system-wide structure 'wants' to behave globally;
- how the 'local' structure 'wants' to behave locally;
- how system-wide and local rationales affect each other.[1]

This step analyzes how the overall structure pushes and pulls on itself in terms of archetypal behavior, how different stakeholders affect different parts of the system, and identifies leverage points within each of these perspectives enriching policy design and implementation. Though any of these tools is insightful by itself, the real power, the systemic power, comes from the multi-dimensional, systemic view they provide when combined.

GLOBAL PERSPECTIVE

The globally rational perspective facilitates understanding of the highest level of expectations for the behavior of the system – what the 'owners' of the system expect. The Managing from Clarity tools provide insight into the feasibility and implications of the desired behavior at the global level. Briefly, the global perspective phase uses three tools. The first, global goal analysis, developed in Chapter 2, determines why the system exists, how that goal is achieved, and how it has behaved over time. We will now discuss the other two tools, archetypes and feedback structure behavior analysis.

Archetypes show how the major positive and negative feedback forces interact at the systemic level, giving insight into generic behavior patterns one should expect to see over time for the entire system. The Feedback Structure Behavior Analysis provides initial quantitative understanding into how key policies affect behavior within the system. Combined, the three analyses at the global perspective deal with upper management's design of the system and its potential for sustainability.

Global goal analysis

Developed in Chapter 2, the global goal analysis uses the key drivers of the global goal to determine the main components of the QualMap, which the rest of the Managing from Clarity methodology analyzes. It is a step in the global perspective because it determines why the 'owners' designed the system in the first place, why it exists, and what results they expect from it.

Archetypes

Archetypes are generic structures of linked feedback loops.[2] These widely studied, generic models provide immediate insight into the potential pathologies of a system and initial ways to correct them.[3]

Dengue case study

In the dengue case study, the archetype analysis in Figure 3.2 shows the structural pattern template for the 'shifting the burden' archetype. In this archetype, a short-term 'solution' is used to correct the problem. As this correction is used increasingly, fundamental long-term corrective measures are used less and less. Over time, the capabilities for the fundamental solution may atrophy or become disabled, leading to even greater reliance on the symptomatic solution, ultimately derailing the sustainability of the system.

The symptoms of this type of behavior are often statements such as, 'These solutions have worked so far. What do you mean there is trouble down that road?' The RBP graphed in Figure 2.4 in

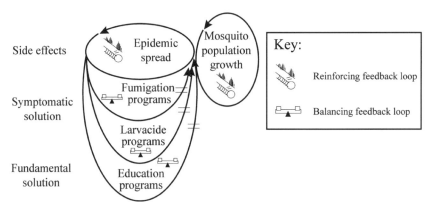

Figure 3.2 Shifting the burden archetype for the dengue case study.

Chapter 2 showed this behavior – outbreaks grow strongly for a while, peak out and then quickly drop off. The archetype teaches that leaders need to focus on the fundamental solution. If the fundamental solution takes a while, use the symptomatic solution to gain time while working on the fundamental solution. Specific to the Secretariat of Health, they should continue fumigation and larvicide intervention programs, while focusing principally on earlier educational programs. Fumigation and larvicide intervention programs are Enabling Resources that control the Value Driving Resources *mosquito population* and *population satisfaction*. *Educational programs* are an Enabling Resource that strongly affects *mosquito population*.

Mint case study

Figure 3.3 shows a high-level or simplified QualMap of the Mint case study that showed one of the more famous systems archetypes – 'Growth and Underinvestment with Drifting Standards.' In this archetype, the Business Cycle is growing quickly as seen in the upswing in product demand. After years of focusing on cost efficiency, however, Mint has delayed reinvestment in new capacity. Though they respond by adding capacity, there is a significant delay in the construction of these facilities, limiting Mint's ability to meet this new demand. At

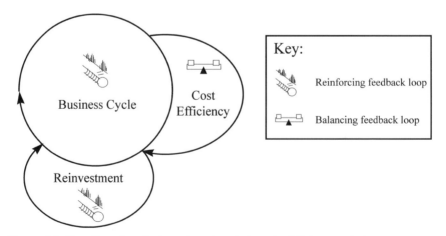

Figure 3.3 Growth and underinvestment archetype for Mint case study.

the same time, customers tighten the standards against which the firm must deliver, demand exceeds normal supply, overburdening and burning out assembly capacity and service quality (the right product at the right time, place and price) slips.

The reference behavior pattern (RBP), in Figure 2.5, reflects this behavior pattern – strong growth in gross revenues and gross costs followed by slower growth in gross revenues and decreasing gross costs. Finding the archetype in the QualMap helps to understand the drivers of the RBP. This archetype teaches that instead of pushing on growth through sales to increase revenues, the company should better understand the drivers that create a market upswing in demand in order. This advanced warning signals timely investment in assembly capacity, helping Mint meet the increasing *customer requirements,* a VDR, and allow growth. This changes the nature of the strategic question being asked at the senior management level, from one of operational effectiveness to systemic insight of industry ebbs and flows. Though simple, this insight is counter intuitive, as evidenced by the number of firms that fall into this systemic trap.

The archetypes have been found to be powerful for managers around the world.[4] The rich story-telling characteristic of the archetypes unlocks some of the key dynamic complexity that leads to counterintuitive behavior in otherwise seemingly familiar systems.

Feedback structure behavior

Feedback Structure Behavior analysis is the third tool used to analyze the QualMap from the global perspective. This analysis helps to understand more quantitatively how a complex system of interrelated reinforcing and compensating feedback loops will behave over time.[5] Though this involves no actual simulation, yet, we can still have an idea of how these systems will tend to behave over time. We have a general idea of this behavior because the archetypal structures of connected feedback loops have been well studied, in both social systems and electromechanical systems. Thus, we do not know precisely how a system will behave without simulation, but we do have an idea of the ways that it can behave. This tool provides a graphical representation of the effects of the combined behaviors over time. Let us begin by putting together the building blocks.

Dengue case study

In the dengue case study, similar structures generate similar behaviors, which is one of the most significant lessons of systems thinking (see Figure 3.4). The reinforcing feedback loop created by the *mosquitoes–larvae–mosquitoes* causal chain, promotes very high growth rates.

Many factors attempt to limit this explosive growth rate of the mosquito population, such as natural climate variability (see Figure 3.5).

Another key population to consider, of course, is the humans that are susceptible, sick and immune. Reviewing the dengue Qual-Map, are the feedback loops pertaining to humans, reinforcing or

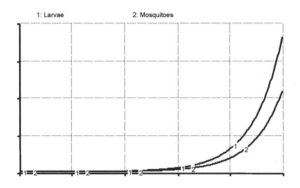

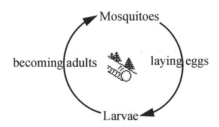

Figure 3.4 Feedback structure behavior analysis for dengue case study.

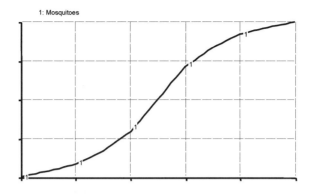

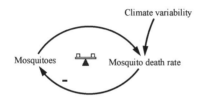

Figure 3.5 Second feedback structure behavior analysis for dengue case study.

compensating? What behavior over time would you expect that structure to generate?[6]

Mint case study

In the Mint case study, the Business Cycle represents the major reinforcing loop of the structure (see Figure 3.6). It suggests that, as *demand* for engines increases, there is a corresponding increase in *engine orders*. Through more orders to supplier, *supplier output* increases, which increases *assembly* as more parts are received. With more assembly, *revenues* from sold orders increase. Reinvesting the profits from the revenues in *product development* makes the product the *right product*, increasing *demand* – positive feedback.[7] In the case where the positive feedback loop is the only feedback mechanism dominating the system, one would expect that *demand*, *engine orders* and *revenues* should all grow exponentially.[8]

The Customer Expectation Cycle represents the minor compensating feedback loop within the major positive feedback loop of the

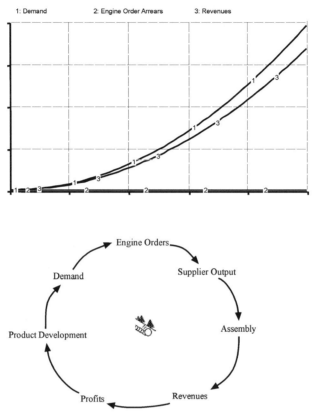

Figure 3.6 Feedback structure behavior analysis for Mint case study.

structure (see Figure 3.7). It suggests that as *demand* for engines increases, *engine orders* increase. For the same level of *assembly*, *engine order arrears* increases, decreasing *revenues*. These reduced profits are not reinvested in *product development*, lessening the probability that ours is the *right product*, decreasing *demand* – negative or balancing feedback.

Combining the reinforcing Business Cycle and the compensating Customer Expectation Cycle provides two interrelated causal feedback loops (see Figure 3.8). This particular combination of positive and negative feedback gives rise to a famous archetype and some very interesting feedback structure behavior. The 'Growth and Under-investment with Drifting Standards' archetype indicates that nothing

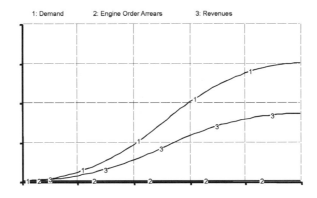

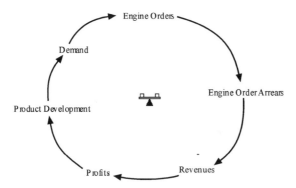

Figure 3.7 Second feedback structure behavior analysis for Mint case study.

will grow forever, since the growth is driven by these limited resources.

The sustainability of a system's growth depends on the management of its growth. This feedback structure creates a 'sigmoidal' or 'S-curve' behavior over time (see Figure 3.8). In the beginning, when resources are plentiful, the Business Cycle promotes the growth of *engine sales* over time. When the resources supporting growth become limited, the customer expectation loop begins to dominate. This compensates the growth in *engine sales* for the lack of on-time delivery experienced through increasing *engine order arrears*. This continues until it reaches a plateau, where the Business Cycle and Customer Expectation Cycle are in equilibrium.

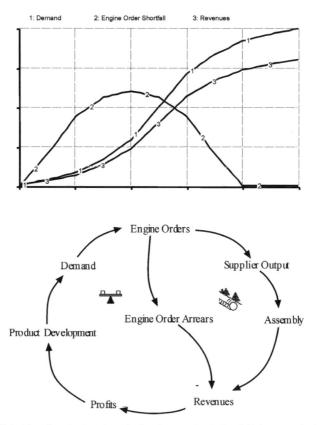

Figure 3.8 Third feedback structure behavior analysis for Mint case study.

The above, optimistic, perspective could also be turned around into a more pessimistic 'overshoot and collapse' behavior (see Figure 3.9). If, instead of taking care of the compensating Customer Expectation Cycle, by focusing effort on on-time delivery, management focused on *demand*, by working harder to sell more engines and by expediting more *engine orders*, the braking force of the compensating loop would grow so strong as to reverse the trend of accelerating growth, in the negative direction – just like a pilot in a death spiral.[9]

The Feedback Structure Behavior tool provides the initial understanding of how the qualitative causal map of interrelated feedback mechanisms may behave. Additionally, when behavior deviates significantly from historical or expected behavior, it prompts one to question the validity of the causal map.

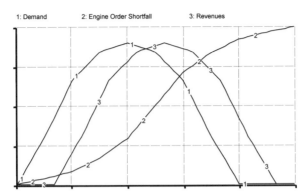

1: Demand   2: Engine Order Shortfall   3: Revenues

Figure 3.9 Fourth feedback structure behavior analysis for Mint case study.

The three global tools

Combining the global goal analysis, archetype, and feedback structure behavior analysis tools provides a significant understanding of the global perspective of the system, as well as strong insights into the system's overall behavior.[10]

Dengue case study

In the dengue case study, the 'shifting the burden' archetype most directly influences the global behavior of the system. The global goal analysis showed that the system existed to minimize morbidity while the RBPs showed the lack of success in achieving that goal. The feedback structure behavior analysis further corroborated the plight by showing how the mosquito population growth engine in the archetype is nearly impossible to control. This global analysis paints a horrifying picture – without a united front, many people will die!

This analysis already shows the crucial nature of cooperation between all the entities involved in the system to minimize lost lives due to dengue. To achieve the fundamental solution will require significant coordination across perspectives, a task that the rest of the Managing from Clarity methodology clarified for the health care officials.

Mint case study

Let us review the results for the Mint case study. The global goal showed that the firm existed to maximize profitability for the owners, while the RBPs showed the lack of success in achieving this goal. The 'Growth and Underinvestment with Drifting Standards' archetype dominates the global perspective. Furthermore, this structure will follow either a sigmoidal or overshoot and collapse behavior over time. At the global level of the system, what picture does this paint?

First, this analysis points out that the management team is not achieving its desired goals. Second, the organization designed by the management team, either through inheritance or its own doing, will not deliver the sustainable growth goals it has set. Third, the unintended consequences of pushing mostly on maintaining market share, through strong sales campaigns, caused management to create whole new structures in the organization, such as expediting, as standard practice, that are only further exacerbating the fundamental problems. In other words, just looking at the global perspective of the QualMap exercise already has provided significant insight into how effective the organization is at achieving the global goals it has set!

Management team dialog

The completion of the global learning analyses provides an excellent opportunity for reflection and dialog. The management team reviews the results of the global perspective of the analysis and develops a list of 'dialog initiation points.' With this list, they begin to think about and record the following:

- the insights that are surfacing;
- the points that would help the team advance their dialog and build a common understanding of the system in question;
- an agreed path forward.

To further complement the global learning, leaders need to understand what is happening at the local level, and what management can do to remedy the current situation, by more effectively designing, managing and leveraging the resources in the system to achieve the global goals. The next two sections consider these two points.

LOCAL PERSPECTIVE

> Fancy what a game of chess would be if all the chessmen had passions and intellects, more or less small and cunning; if you were not only uncertain about your adversary's men, but a little uncertain also about your own; if your knight could shuffle himself onto a new square by the sly; if your bishop, in disgust at your castling, could wheedle your pawns out of their places; and if your pawns, hating you because they are pawns, could make away from their appointed posts that you might get checkmate on a sudden. You might be the longest-headed of the deductive reasoners, and yet you might be beaten by your own pawns. You would be especially likely to be beaten, if you depended arrogantly on your mathematical imagination, and regarded your passionate pieces with contempt.
>
> (George Eliot, *Felix Holt, The Radical*, 1980, p. 237)

No matter how clear the organization is about its global goal, nothing will happen if the local goals are not aligned to achieve that global goal. This section provides a perspective that has clarified for many decision-makers, what the local goals are and how to align them to achieve the global goal.

The local perspective looks at each of the sub-systems and the drivers of the behavior they exhibit. The Managing from Clarity tools provide significant insight into the implications and consistency of the desired behavior for each group within the system. The locally rational phase presents the Systemic Stakeholders' View and the Trend Analysis, which are used to understand the local rationale within each of the subsystems.

Systemic stakeholders' view

> We never realized how strong our functional blinders were. We get so into our own part of the business, we don't even realize how we affect other groups.
>
> (A capital equipment manufacturer)

Further analysis of the QualMap provides insight into the key factors that affect departmental performance and provide a basis for reconfiguring departmental performance indicators. The Systemic Stakeholders'

View, which overlays the QualMap with organizational or departmental boundaries, often highlights points of conflict where one department has strong influence on resources affecting another department far down (or up) the business chain. Departments share resources, at the interface between them. These shared resources become candidates for sharing responsibility between the departments. These boundaries often have severe implications, minimizing communication among groups that share the same Enabling Resources.

The Systemic Stakeholders' View is elicited from the different stakeholders affected by the system being modeled. Lines drawn over the QualMap show what stakeholders are directly responsible for those resources. Further, the locally rational goal(s) of each stakeholder are included to reflect the basic intent of the stakeholder responsible for those resources.

Dengue case study

The Systemic Stakeholders' View of the dengue case study shows (see Figure 3.10) that the four principal participants in the system have locally rational objectives, yet the conflict between the participants becomes clear. They are all concerned with different attributes of the problem! Sick people want special attention, while doctors have too many patients to give significant individualized care. Municipal

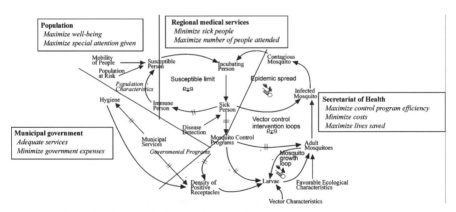

Figure 3.10 Systemic stakeholders' view for dengue case study.

governments have very limited budgets for medical services, while the Secretariat of Health attempts to maximize lives saved.

Mint case study

Revisiting the Mint Case Study with the Systemic Stakeholders' View, Figure 3.11 identifies how each group within the organization has what seem to be very rational, local goals. However, when the management team saw, for the first time, the goals explicitly expressed within the high-level QualMap, they recognized this local rationality created strong global conflicts.[11]

In this case, the strong incentives for maintaining market share pushed Marketing to sell as much as possible in the growing market, aggressively competing for the large profits per unit. On the other hand, the years of experience in downsizing and optimizing capacity had taught Assembly to focus on minimizing overall production costs. These seemingly obvious local goals created a counter-intuitive conflict at the global level. This high-level QualMap shows that as sales increase faster than assembly can adjust its capacity, the number of late orders begins to increase.[12] Already this shows that two seemingly logical rationales (sell as much as possible and minimize production costs) have created serious communication barriers

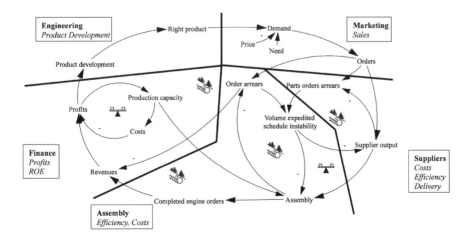

Figure 3.11 Systemic stakeholders' view for Mint case study.

between the two groups. The end of the global perspective analysis explores the implications for the global perspective that these analytical tools provide for these case studies.

Trend analysis

Trend analysis uncovers the local level expectations and understandings for behavior of each of the resources within the subsystem. At the local level, managers work with resources that enable (Enabling Resources) the accumulation and maintenance of the Value-Driving Resources. This analysis depends heavily on the team members representing the expert knowledge of each subsystem. These experts from each subsystem tend to have a tremendous amount of detailed knowledge about how their area works; however, when identifying the variables to include in the model, the team will need to aggregate much of this activity. As such, the individual Enabling Resources, or variables in the model, tend to represent not single resources, but rather entire parts of the subsystem. Those involved in the daily operation of the local subsystem have different initiatives, measurement systems, and expectations for each of the variables identified within their subsystem.

The Trend Analysis captures these local understandings and expectations and checks the consistency of the interrelated expectations. For example, people want educational levels to increase, and they want to lessen taxes, while they do not want to take the enormous burden of rethinking how to make the whole education process more efficient and effective – inconsistent policies and expectations.

In the Trend Analysis, the facilitators elicit the historical trends for each resource in the model, as well as the expectations for the future behavior of the resource. Within systems, some resources require significant changes in the future direction, within the range of an order of magnitude, as compared with historical behavior. For example, inventory costs might be increasing strongly and the desired trend would be for them to be decreasing significantly. Other resources may actually require little change. From a systemic viewpoint, this becomes significant because the way in which the resources are connected implies that a single change in one resource will have multiple effects on other resources, some of which may not have been desired.

Trend Analysis also checks the internal consistency of a group of arguments. In other words, do all the stated directions in which people are proposing to move the resources, unite into a coherent, consistent overall picture? Does the local view of each resource agree with the global system purpose? Does the story make sense?

One petroleum client wanted to convert their research and development arm into a cutting-edge, world leader in technology innovation. Though definitely a strategic advantage, the QualMap and Trend Analysis showed that creating this capacity was impossible within the structure of this business and its relative place within the industry. This exercise led the management team to revise its research and development strategy to fit what they agreed was feasible, plans that focused on developing capacity in acquiring and assimilating cutting-edge technology developed by their competitors.

The Trend Analysis is generated through interviews with the stakeholders of the system that discuss each resource in the model, its current trend and the direction the team wants the trend to head in the future. For clarity, the team is limited to describing these trends as Constant, Increasing, Decreasing, Significantly Increasing, or Significantly Decreasing.

Dengue case study
From the dengue case study (see Table 3.1), historically the system's behavior is quite different from that desired for the future. For example, in the past, there have been outbreaks, and, clearly, the people do not want more outbreaks in the future. For each variable in the table, the team looks for major gaps in performance between the current and desired state. For example, the chart indicates that the team wants *Adult Mosquitoes* to reduce significantly. Returning to the QualMap, what causal connections are there to this variable

Table 3.1 Trend table for dengue case study.

Resources	Current	Desired
Adult mosquitoes	I	SD
Contagious mosquito	I	SD
Density of positive receptacles	I	D
Disease detection	C	SI
Favorable ecological characteristics	C	C
Hygiene	C	I
Immune person	I	D
Incubating person	C	C
Infected mosquito	I	D
Larvae	I	D
Mobility of people	C	C
Mosquito control programs	C	I
Municipal services	C	C
Population at risk	I	D
Sick person	I	SD
Susceptible person	I	D
Vector characteristics	C	C

Notes: C = constant, D = decreasing, I = increasing, S = significant

and in what direction are they expected to go in the future? This is how to check the internal consistency of the QualMap, as well as expose inconsistencies in team member's assumptions about the system.

For example, what are the costs of radically improving disease detection and drastically reducing the numbers of mosquitoes? Are these funds available, and is this the most economic way to achieve the goal of zero deaths? Is this feasible?

Mint case study

As can be seen from Table 3.2, many of the current trends require significant changes in order to achieve the direction and magnitude that the management team wants. Hopefully by now, an understanding of what it means to make changes in an existing system should cause little light bulbs and alarms to go off in your head. To achieve the desired change in the behavior of these resources will require changes to the structure or incentives that are generating that behavior. The changes required for each resource will most probably affect the ability to achieve the desired trend in the other resources, thus one needs to check the consistency of these changes.

Table 3.2 Trend table for Mint case study.

Resources	Current	Desired
Assembly inventory	C	D
Assembly remaining capacity	C	I
Assembly throughput	C	I
Correct component mix	C	C
Costs	I	SD
Hire supplier labor	C	SI
Materials carrying cost	I	SD
Profits	D	I
Reinvestment	C	I
Engine R&O work	C	I
Schedule instability	I	SD
Spares orders scheduled	C	I
Supplier labor	C	SI
Supplier labor productivity	C	I
Supplier output	C	I
Supplier production capacity	C	I
Supplier remaining capacity	C	C
Volume expedited	I	SD

Notes: C = constant, D = decreasing, I = increasing, S = significant

By returning to the QualMap for the Mint case study, one can 'walk through' the causal chains to see if the desired future changes are consistent. For example, Table 3.2 suggests increasing *assembly capacity* and decreasing *inventory*, while decreasing *costs*, which have been increasing. During the trend analysis exercise, this discrepancy brings up the interesting questions, 'How are *costs* going to decrease while increasing *assembly capacity* and carrying less *inventory*? What effects will less *inventory* have on *assembly throughput* and *schedule instability*? What are the underlying assumptions that would let this be achieved? Are these assumptions realistic?'

The level of questions this local-level consistency check raises has provided insight for leaders in understanding the feasibility and interrelatedness of local-level objectives, incentives and actions, and has often led to significant changes in strategic planning for the organization.

GLOBAL GOALS ANALYSIS, REVISITED

At the beginning of this chapter, the team stated and mapped its understanding of the *stated* goals and subgoals of the system. Insight has been gained into the variables that generate leverage. Now the *actual* goals and subgoals discovered during the GRASP process need to be mapped. These will measure the structural leverage that the goal alignment provides.

By examining the actual subgoals of each feedback subsystem and their relationships to form higher-level goals, one can develop, through a system goals network, an understanding of what the actual goal of the system is. This bottom-up actual analysis will be compared with the top-down stated analysis. Teams will almost always be surprised at the differences between actual and stated goals in two key measures: (1) goal alignment – are the subgoals working synergistically or antagonistically?; and (2) domination of unwritten rules of the game – the level to which the stated and actual goals are different.[13] The underlying assumption here is that misaligned goals, as analyzed in the actual and stated System Goals Networks, will not allow leaders to achieve their goals, consistently and sustainably.

Dengue case study

In the dengue case study, the *stated* system goals network was developed in Chapter 2 (redrawn here as Figure 3.12). The *actual* system goals network can be derived from the system-wide discovery analysis (see Figure 3.13).

Figure 3.13 shows that insufficient investment and limited capabilities in *public hygiene* and *medical facilities* actually caused the *mosquito*

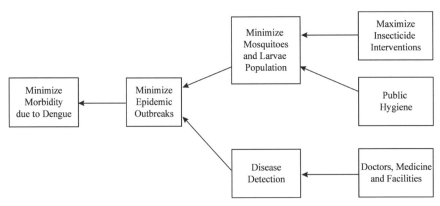

Figure 3.12 'Stated' global means–ends analysis for dengue case study.

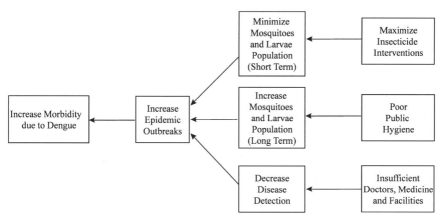

Figure 3.13 'Actual' global means–ends analysis for dengue case study.

population to increase and decrease the ability of the medical services to detect the disease – thus the set of strategies the Secretariat of Health traditionally used to attack the epidemic provided low leverage.

Mint case study

In the Mint case study, the *stated* system goals network (redrawn here as Figure 3.14) showed a profit-maximizing firm. The *actual* system goals network (see Figure 3.15) tells a very different story.

The global goal was sustainable high profitability, the initial state of profitability was low, and the actual state of profitability worsened – thus, the strategy, as defined by the global goal and subgoals, provided very low leverage. As Marketing's policy of *Maximizing units sold* and Assembly's policy of *minimizing unit cost* combine, they inadvertently

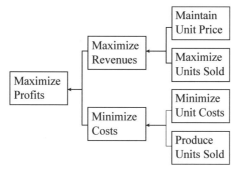

Figure 3.14 'Stated' global means–ends analysis for Mint case study.

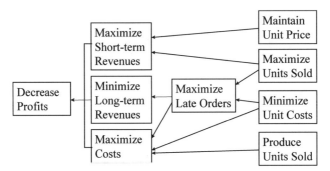

Figure 3.15 'Actual' global means–ends analysis for Mint case study.

cause the system to *maximize late orders*, as described earlier in the case study. This unintended consequence drives down *revenues* and increases *costs*.

The global to local gap

Having completed both the global and local level analyses, one can compare the vision that the two perspectives provide.[14] From the global perspective, Value-Driving Resources primarily exist within reinforcing feedback loops (i.e., the business growth cycle), with the explicit purpose of continuously creating value for the system's 'owners.' Furthermore, from the local perspective, management of Enabling Resources (i.e., assembly capacity) primarily exists within balancing feedback loops, with the explicit purpose of utilizing these resources as efficiently as possible. This paradox of a system where the global goal focuses on growth and the local goals focus on stability is the 'global to local paradox.'

Global to local paradox

The two very different perspectives naturally fight each other, with one trying to grow and the other trying to stabilize. Let us dig a little deeper to understand some of the significant implications of this paradox. If management at the local perspective lives primarily in a world of balancing feedback, they focus on those actions that close the gap between the actual state and the desired state. Further-more, in balancing feedback systems, this management would only focus on closing the gap, because by doing so they are doing the right job, since the desired goal is the correct one, by definition.

The global to local paradox shows, among other things, a key reason for the resistance to change in systems. Upper management expects change, but middle and lower management are structured to resist it. To achieve growth that satisfies the ever-increasing Stakeholder Goals, upper management expects the Value-Driving Resources to grow exponentially, by allowing growth through periodic, step-change investments in Enabling Resources.[15] However, as the Value-Driving Resources grow exponentially, they require ever greater step-change increases in the Enabling Resources. As management at the local perspective spends more time on changing and, correspondingly, relatively less time on Enabling Resource efficiency, they become more frustrated (their culture promotes stability, not change) and limits their ability to manage development of the Enabling Resource.[16]

'CURRENT STATE' ASSESSMENT

Comparing the global and the local perspectives assesses the 'current state' of the system. These two perspectives have focused the team's attention on why the system exists, the resources and actions that are in place to achieve the global goal, how the whole system is struc-tured, and how peoples' rationales affect the system's behavior. This provides a systemic view of the system's current state. This assessment highlights and makes explicit the potential gaps between the owners' desires and what the system is structured to deliver. With this assess-ment, leaders now have specific ideas of what they need to do to close the gap in the system's ability to achieve the global goal. Samples of the 'current state' assessment follow.

Dengue case study

In the dengue case study, the global perspective showed that the Mexican Secretariat of Health faced a 'shifting the burden' archetype, where the tendency is to focus on short-term solutions instead of the fundamental solution. The well-intentioned goals of the numerous areas attacking the dengue issue were based on significantly different incentives, thus frustrating overall epidemic management. Some experts focused on medical diagnosis and treatment, while others focused on mosquito eradication and others on education and hygiene. The short-term focus and lack of communication amongst interest groups lead to entrenched and conflicting opinions of how to control the epidemic best.

This multitude of intervention policies led to strong political in-fighting among the interest groups to obtain their share of the very limited financial resources available. Worse still, for the public at large, the well-intentioned efforts of all of the different groups combined still permitted periodic outbreaks. These findings are summarized in the 'Current State' Assessment in Table 3.3.

Table 3.3 'Current state' assessment for dengue case study.
Global Goal: *Minimize lives lost and costs*

GRASP level	Conflict
Stakeholder goals	Fundamental differences in 'the right approach' generated in-fighting and poor communication among policy advisors and policy makers. This led to a focus on short-term solution thinking in order to get a piece of the limited budget. The risk to the public was not diminished.
Value-driving resources	Different incentives for the individuals exist at each of the multiple intervention points creating a different language at each point for controlling dengue. Little attention is paid to public awareness programs as dengue is viewed as a medical problem. More effort is spent on educating doctors, taking more time away from their patients. The government agency has limited funds and will have to cut back on other important programs to focus on dengue. This is only feasible if an epidemic is already underway.
Enabling resources	Fumigation and larvicide brigades show the public that the government is 'doing something' about dengue, but the effectiveness is limited. More effective chemicals cost significantly more. Detection infrastructure is poor and expensive to implement. The doctor-to-patient ratio does not permit much extra time for dengue diagnosis.

These global and local perspectives led to the preliminary conclusion that the Secretariat's ability to move the system in the desired direction was low. The Secretariat needed an objective, non-partisan perspective of the system and of the multiple intervention points, to understand better how to apply its scarce resources to limiting such a dangerous disease. Analyzing the local perspective uncovered the internal logic behind these assumptions and paradigms and provided a mechanism and a common language for these experts to discuss their ideas.

The local level perspective showed that the issue at hand was the need to make explicit the underlying, implicit assumptions and paradigms that shaped each participant's view of the 'right' solution. Through this effort, they recognized that each of the alternatives had significantly different time dimensions and that each of the groups within the Secretariat's team had very different aims. This provided an initial framework for analyzing epidemic control.

Further analysis showed a multitude of potential intervention points in the system. Some of these issues required relatively little effort, and others required significant investments over time. All required significant changes that had to be implemented and managed with very limited financial resources. At last, the entire team was talking about controlling dengue on the same terms.

Mint case study

In the Mint case study, the global perspective showed that the management team faces a 'Growth and Underinvestment with Drifting Standards' archetype. While pushing sales and fighting late orders with expediters, they should be increasing assembly capacity and throughput to assuage future problems in on-time delivery. These issues arise from the organizational structure and the incentives management used to measure success. Though management was hoping to see their actions increase sales, they were more probably pushing themselves into an overshoot and collapse behavior.

The local perspective shows that departmental management is trying to design significant changes in their local resources, and that

Table 3.4 'Current state' assessment for Mint case study.

Global Goal: *Maximize profits*

GRASP level	Conflict
Stakeholder goals	Sales puts orders into the process faster than Assembly's capacity to produce the orders, not meeting Sales' delivery promises. Finance wants to wait for increased profits before investing in greater Assembly capacity.
Value-driving resources	Sales creates more orders than can be fulfilled on time, frustrating their ability to sell. Assembly focuses on efficient capacity utilization and highly trained technicians, yet is under staffed with long delays to bring new technicians up to speed. Finance has to provide high returns to investors, but needs to invest heavily and quickly, adding great risk in a cyclical market.
Enabling resources	To increase sales now, the Sales group promises delivery terms that Assembly cannot meet. To meet delivery terms for critical orders, Assembly expedites those orders. To decrease financial risk of investment in capacity, Finance leans on its suppliers and on internal cost reduction.

there are inconsistencies between the locally rational goals of different departments. They are all still in a cost-reduction mode, and just beginning to talk about improved customer maintenance. These findings are summarized in the 'Current state' assessment in Table 3.4.

These global and local perspectives led to the preliminary conclusion that the relatively quick upswing in industry demand caught the cost-reduction-focused management by surprise. Currently management's ability to move its system in the desired direction is low. The department and incentive structures reinforce the poor communication between the departments, causing them to suffer performance setbacks. This prompted the departments to react by intentionally damaging the performance of other areas in an attempt to fix quickly their own problems – Marketing accelerating the rate of units sold knowing that Production cannot increase its output as quickly. This was a difficult, dynamic, and probably not unique, situation to manage. This analysis provides a rich source of dialog initiation points for discussing the paradigms that are limiting the management team as well as the potential corporate design issues that need to be tackled.

CHAPTER LEARNING SUMMARY

Evaluating what was learned in this chapter, the global and local learning loops provided two very different perspectives of the same system. As was stated in Chapter 1, this has provided a new understanding of the system, as well as increasing one's ability to communicate this understanding. Chapter 4 will complete the GRASP Map and Analysis of the QualMap, considering the third component, the system manager's integrative perspective. This perspective will assess the desired 'end state' of the system, and how management can leverage the system in that direction.

Management's Job: Integrating the Local Perspectives to Achieve the Global Perspective

4

> We all agreed that our system was completely at odds with itself. Going through the Managing from Clarity Integrative process gave us confidence in how we would go forward, as a team, to achieve the global goal.
>
> (An executive in the telecommunications industry)

The integrative perspective views the system from the viewpoint of the system manager, who has been charged with accomplishing the global goals, set out by the system owners.[1] Figuratively, this role is like that of the orchestra conductor, in that, with this responsibility, the system manager has access to the owner's resources, and the authority to design, implement and maintain a system of tactical objectives and policies with which to carry out these goals. From the integrative perspective, this framework provides the system manager with four main insights into resource performance:

1 The influence and exposure of each resource in the system (Resource Influence and Exposure Analysis).
2 The differences in perceived relationship expectations between different groups in the organization (Stakeholder Relationship Analysis).
3 The effects current performance indicators have on the inter-relationships among the subsystems, and the determination of appropriate performance indicators (Performance Indicator Analysis).

4   How changes in the causal link and delay structure might enhance or hamper achievement of system-wide goals (Structural and Delay Analysis).

RESOURCE INFLUENCE AND EXPOSURE ANALYSIS[2]

The first step on the road to this deeper understanding is to determine the relative importance of each variable with respect to the other variables in the system being modeled, as captured in the QualMap. The Resource Influence and Exposure Analysis establishes this relative importance of each variable. The methodology was developed by Michel Godet, and is referred to as MICMAC, French for Cross-Impact Matrix Multiplication Applied to Classification.

In many organizations, participants often state that they need to change how a variable behaves – 'we need to increase sales, and increase labor productivity.' Yet, as leaders and managers, it is often impossible to directly affect a variable, such as 'sales,' because the results are dependent upon a host of interrelated activities. The focus of this analysis, using the QualMap as the source, is to determining the closest variables that can be manipulated that will give the highest impact on the variables that need to move in the desired direction. It is important to remember that the QualMap is an integration of the variables deemed to be most relevant and important by the decision-makers of the organization and not a detailed list of the operational variables.

The ability to change the behavior of a variable over time depends significantly on the variable's exposure to other variables in the system and their corresponding behavior. It is non-intuitive in dynamically complex systems which variables provide the most systemic leverage in achieving the desired system behavior.

Moreover, intuitive solutions to dynamically complex problems often lead to exactly the wrong solution! The MICMAC tool identifies those variables with the greatest influence and exposure in the system being studied. Influence refers to the relative degree to which one variable impacts the rest. Exposure refers to the relative degree by which all other variables affect each variable.

Within the multitude of Value-Driving and Enabling Resources comprising the QualMap, leaders know they need to focus attention on those resources that provide the most leverage within the system. This is Archimedes' principle. Leverage is determined by how easy a variable is to move (exposure), and how much effect it has on the system when it is moved (influence). The MICMAC analysis identifies the relative impact and exposure each variable has compared to the others in the system. The output of the MICMAC analysis is the 2 × 2 matrix in Figure 4.1, which differentiates means (drivers) and ends (dependent) resources.

The horizontal axis *Influence* illustrates the relative, normalized degree in which any change in a resource affects the system's behavior.[3] The vertical axis *Exposure* illustrates the relative degree in which any change in the system affects the behavior of a resource. The matrix has four quadrants, as described in Table 4.1.[4] Though the figure clearly demarcates four sectors, points found close to two different sectors (those on the borders) could just as easily be interpreted to be in a nebulous zone between sectors. The point is to understand how to look at the variable, not to pinpoint the sector to which it belongs.

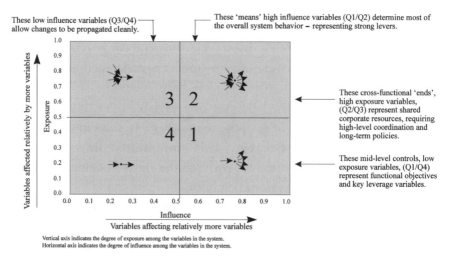

Figure 4.1 Resource influence and exposure analysis.

Table 4.1 MICMAC matrix quadrant details.

Quadrant	Exposure and Influence	Description
1 Dispersing Resources	Exposure – Low Influence – High	Dispersing ends and means variables affect many strategic ends and means but are exposed to few of them. These tend to be variables where managers can actually intervene. Changes to these variables tend to influence the behavior of the system.
2 Linking Resources	Exposure – High Influence – High	Linking strategic ends and means variables are both highly exposed and highly influential. These tend to be variables that managers cannot affect directly because they require significant coordination of effort among multiple resources. They transmit the effects of changes in a strategy design throughout a causal network of ends and means. Due to their strong relation with the whole system, these variables tend to be very unstable, strongly affecting feedback effects. A low number of these variables indicates a relatively stable system.
3 Absorbing Resources	Exposure – High Influence – Low	Absorbing strategic ends and means variables affect a few ends and means, but are exposed to many. These variables tend to be system outputs that show the results of many interrelated actions, thus they are strong indicators of the system's health. They depict ends met through multiple means, but their high exposure makes them vulnerable even to small changes in a QualMap.
4 Singular Resources	Exposure – Low Influence – Low	Singular ends and means variables allow changes to be propagated cleanly, without any repercussions for the rest of the QualMap.

The results from this analysis provide three key insights, at this stage:

1   A method for understanding the leverage implicit within the structure of the system.

2   A classification of who should be managing what resources, and the level of coordination required to determine the consequences of the variable's movement.

3   A test of the validity of the QualMap. If the results do not make sense, one of two things has happened: (a) confirming from the QualMap that the relationships are correct establishes a common understanding of the key interrelationships that drive the system's behavior; and (b) if the relationships are wrong, the validity of a qualitative map has been tested and this requires revising the QualMap and running the MICMAC analysis again.

With a validated QualMap and the resulting MICMAC analysis data, these results can be applied to the problem at hand. Making explicit and understanding the underlying structure, key relationships, and the direction and magnitude of the change desired for each variable, the implications these results have on the existing policies can be dis-covered. Keep in mind that the following comments regarding policy significance and policy attack are the result of many deep discussions with the management team. Often the policy significance and attack seem very obvious and simple, afterward, often obscuring the painful path of heated debate that has taken the team to this clarity.

Dengue case study

For the dengue case study, Figure 4.2 demonstrates the results of the MICMAC analysis. About 20% of the variables fall in the high influ-ence quadrants #1 and #2.[5] This typical distribution is to be expected, as there are a relatively smaller number of resources that strongly influ-ence the rest of the variables. For clarification, this matrix and analysis indicate nothing of a resource's absolute importance in a system, rather the focus is on the relative influence resources have on the movement of other resources.[6]

Reviewing the results often provides interesting responses from the management team. Some of the results confirm prior beliefs and some disprove them. In the dengue case study, the three resources with high influence and low exposure, *disease detection, mosquito control programs*

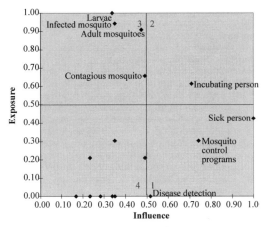

Figure 4.2 MICMAC output for dengue case study.

and *sick people*, represent the prime targets recommended by the epidemiological control experts, confirming the understanding from the QualMap.

What did the MICMAC results imply for the Mexican Secretary of Health and his team? First, identify the key resource in each quadrant, then apply the characteristics of the Trend Analysis that variables in each quadrant tend to display, and evaluate potential plans for change in the current policy (see Table 4.2).

Although the MICMAC process confirmed the teams' understanding of the key relationships in combating dengue (they had not learned anything new yet, they just saw what they knew in a more focused and, more importantly, prioritized context), the MICMAC results prompted the team to reassess what to do with each of the three critical variables in Quadrant #1. No single approach would be sufficient to achieve the goal. The exercise provided a forum for generating consensus about what issues had to be discussed jointly and why. This proved to be valuable to the effectiveness of the team in agreeing on an integrated solution that fell within the very limited budget.

Mint case study

Figure 4.3 presents the MICMAC analysis results for the Mint case study. Though none of the variables in Quadrant #1 surprised the

Table 4.2 MICMAC analysis for dengue case study.[7]

Policy analysis: Dengue case study

Quadrant #1: Dispersing Resources (Quick Leverage)
Resources: *disease detection, mosquito control programs, sick person*

Policy significance	These governmental and regional 'means' enabling variables are relatively easy to change due to relative independence.
Policy attack	Require integrated, preventive and control governmental policies.
Dialog initiation points	Quick wins: Are extensive *fumigation* and *larvicide control programs* required in order to prevent an epidemic outbreak? How does initial implementation date of control programs affect their success rate? Sustainable actions: Would educating the people to clean up the refuse halt *Mosquito population* growth? Would extensive training of regional doctors lead to better disease detection, treatment, and isolation?

Quadrant #2: Linking Resources (Complex Leverage)
Resource: *incubating person*

Policy significance	This enabling variable is difficult to change due to its high exposure to multiple variables; exponential growth of its effects within the system; and difficult detection.
Policy attack	To achieve the desired significant change in this variable requires coordinated and integrated proactive operational-level policies directed at the enabling resource.
Dialog initiation points	Quick wins: Is it possible to prevent *sick people* from entering the country? Would early warning of the medical staff in the high-risk regions prevent exponential epidemic spread? Who needs to be involved in the *disease detection programs*? Sustainable actions: Would medical staff training be necessary to improve policy's effectiveness? What current, implicit incentives might prevent regional medical staff from detecting the disease early on?

Quadrant #3: Absorbing Resources (Summary Indicators)
Resources: *adult mosquitoes, contagious mosquitoes, infected mosquitoes, larvae*

Policy significance	These operational 'ends' variables are difficult to change due to their exponential growth within the system, and due to the desired significant changes and their high exposure to multiple variables.
Policy attack	To curtail the *mosquito population* explosion requires an integrated, well-coordinated, multi-pronged attack.
Dialog initiation points	Quick wins: Is there a short-term policy, besides *larvicide* and *fumigation* interventions, to halt *mosquito population* growth? Who needs to be directly involved in the implementation of mosquito eradication programs? Sustainable actions: Is there an effective, outbreak isolation policy or is it necessary to implement several policies? Would policies that remove the fertile reproductive areas for *larvae* reproduction halt *mosquito population* growth?

Quadrant #4: Singular Resources (Potentially Low Impact/Low Leverage)
Resources: The remaining variables

Policy significance	These tactical, external and internal variables affect organizational information and material flow. Due to the relatively low interrelationship with the system, these variables should be lower priority change items.
Policy attack	Require periodic review during change programs to ensure that they do not restrict change of higher priority variables, and that change policies are affecting them in the expected direction.

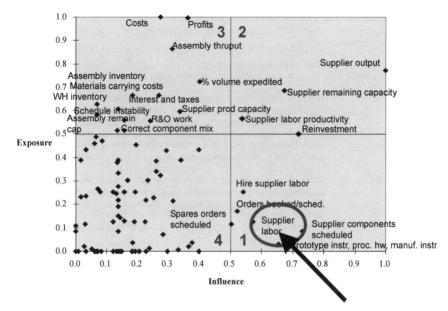

Figure 4.3 MICMAC output for mint case study.

management team as to their relative influence, further probing generated great shock when the team realized what level of management was responsible for these critical resources. For example, the issue of *supplier labor*, seen below in Quadrant #1 (highly influential) was managed by a three-person team of entry-level analysts! This resulted from the firm's 'two arms distance' attitude toward suppliers, which evolved during five years of cost cutting and outsourcing initiatives.[8]

Again, combining the Trend Analysis for each variable and its relative influence and exposure in the system from the MICMAC analysis, let us take a closer look at the policy significance and routes for attack for this case (see Table 4.3).

The MICMAC analysis provides unique insight into the variables that will leverage the ability to both get the system going in the right direction, with quick wins, and keep the system going over time, with sustainable actions. Additionally, thoughtful consideration of the 'Dialog Initiation Points' increases overall shared understanding and management of the most critical components of the system.

Table 4.3 MICMAC analysis for Mint case study.

Policy analysis: Mint case study

Quadrant #1: Dispersing Resources (Quick Leverage)
Resources: *prototype instructions, supplier labor, supplier components scheduled, orders booked and scheduled*

Policy significance	These supplier-output related tactical variables affect system behavior significantly due to high influence, and are relatively easy to change due to relative independence. To achieve the expected trend requires important structural changes from the current trend, mainly, change the level of management that is responsible for these variables.
Policy attack	Well-defined, coordinated, tactical-level policies ensure that changes result in desired effects throughout the system.
Dialog initiation points	Quick wins: Strengthen information visibility between sales and suppliers. Look for possible quick supplier productivity gains. Sustainable actions: Completely restructure supplier relationship. Need to help suppliers develop continuous improvement programs. Are the short-term and long-term results of these actions consistent with corporate goals?

Quadrant #2: Linking Resources (Complex Leverage)
Resources: *reinvestment, supplier output, supplier remaining capacity, supplier labor productivity*

Policy significance	These division-level strategic enabling variables are highly interrelated with corporate-level and supplier strategies, thus difficult to change independently. The desired change in these key growth-risk variables requires significant strategic planning, most probably with suppliers.
Policy attack	Management needs to rethink the current strategy in achieving production flexibility and technology increases (drifting standards) against the 7-year cycle demand.
Dialog initiation points	Quick wins: Improved communication with suppliers will prepare them to respond better to sales needs. Sustainable actions: Supplier output and growth capacity should play a significant role in corporate strategic management.

Quadrant #3: Absorbing Resources (Summary Leverage)
Resources: *costs, profits, assembly throughput, % volume expedited, assembly inventory, materials carrying costs, warehouse inventory, interest and taxes, supplier production capacity, repair and overhaul work, correct component mix, assembly remaining capacity, schedule instability*

Policy significance	These value-driving resources and enabling variables are highly exposed to multiple variables, which makes it difficult to change significantly the system's behavior with single variable policies. Most of these variables require significant change in their current trend, if the company is to remain a competitive player.
Policy attack	Require interrelated top-level policies integrated across operating lines to change behavior.
Dialog initiation points	Quick wins: Increased information visibility will increase stability, removing some of the braking force. Sustainable actions: Need to rethink the whole capacity change and information flow process.

Quadrant #4: Singular Resources (Potentially Low Leverage)
Resources: The remaining variables

Policy significance	These exogenous and mid-level policy variables represent client internal decision controls. Relatively they have low interrelationship with the system so they should be lower priority change items.
Policy attack	Require periodic review during change programs to ensure that they do not restrict change of higher priority variables, and that change policies are affecting them in the expected direction.

STAKEHOLDER RELATIONSHIP ASSESSMENT

This analysis looks further at the specific relationships among the main players in the system. In this regard, relationships include multiple facets, from supplier to customer, from independent to shared resources, and from alliances to conflicts. The Stakeholder Relationship Assessment describes the relationship that exists between the different actors in the system, from each of their perspectives. This analysis highlights convergences and divergences as well as potential for alliances and conflicts between different actors sharing common resources and incentives within the system.

Most relationships between departments or subsystems are reciprocal. In generic terms, in some cases, I am the supplier and you are the client. At other times in the relationship, you are the supplier and I am the client. An initial assessment of these relationships, provides insight from three perspectives:

1   What each group thinks they are trying to achieve (their Objectives and main Problems).
2   How each group sees their relationships with the other groups in the system (Supplier and Customer relationships).
3   The differences in perception from one group to another, on the same supplier and customer relationships.

In organizations, the blame for problems often accompanies misaligned perceptions. This exercise makes the perceptions of those relationship perceptions explicit, so that they can be examined. It also makes explicit the effect differences in perception have on the behavior of the overall system. This provides a crucial step in the design of effective systems.

Dengue case study

Table 4.4 shows how, from the first perspective (objectives and problems), each subsystem's objective makes sense locally, and that they face difficult issues because of actions from different subsystems; for example, the Municipal Government feel that they are doing everything

Table 4.4 Stakeholder relationship assessment for dengue case study.

	Perception of their supplier and client relationship with these groups			
	Secretary of Health	Regional Medical Services	Population	Municipal Government
Secretary of Health	O: Effective disease control P: Not enough time and financial resources for too many interventions points and cities	S: We provide the budget C: They do not identify the disease in time for us to intervene SR: Budget, relevant knowledge	S: We want to have a healthy population and eradicate illness C: They do not have hygiene SR: Population health	S: No relationship C: The towns do not have appropriate running water and refuse pick up services SR: Municipal services
Regional Medical Services	S: We report epidemics incidents as soon as we identify them C: They always give us fewer resources than we need SR: Budget, relevant information	O: Maintain the population health P: Limited medical resources (human and material)	S: I want to assist and cure all the people C: When they feel bad, they do not come immediately SR: Population health	S: I control population diseases C: They provide adequate services to the clinics, but inadequate ones to the population SR: Population Health, municipal services
Population	S: No relationship C: People from the Secretary of Health come just when there are troubles SR: Epidemic control programs	S: I put my health in the doctor's hands C: They cure us, give us medicines and send us home SR: Population health	O: Be happy and healthy with my family P: Constant epidemic outbreaks and other diseases	S: I select the government C: They do not provide us with running water or refuse pickup SR: Municipal services
Municipal government	S: No relationship C: They control epidemics through control programs SR: Epidemic control programs	S: I provide municipal services to the clinics C: A lot of people are getting sick SR: Municipal services, population health	S: As a management figure, I provide services for the population to live more comfortably C: They always ask for more SR: Municipal services	O: Fulfill service needs and maintain a healthy political environment P: Not enough financial resources for multiple needs

Key: O = Objective, P = Problem, S = Supplier, C = Client, SR = Shared Resources that they can for their community, with the limited resources they are given. However, Municipal Government continually fights with insufficient resources to solve difficult demands, often exacerbating their two clients, the Population and National Government, in the process.

From the second perspective (supplier and customer relationships), many subsystems perceive the same supplier and client relationships differently. For example, the Population perceives that, as a supplier, they provide Municipal Government with a job and taxes, and that, as a client, their needs are not met by the services the Municipal Government provides. On the other hand, Municipal Government perceives that they have very limited financial resources to work with in providing expensive services to the Population, and that, as a client, they receive many complaints, insufficient taxes, and too few suggestions from the Population that elected them.

From the third perspective (comparing the two interpretations), this misalignment ensures that the Population and Municipal Government have practically no means of communicating with each other, even though their relationship directly affects at least two key resources – *medical services provided* and *financial resources*.

Mint case study

Table 4.5 shows how, starting with the first perspective (objectives and problems), each subsystem has an objective that from their local perspective makes sense, and that the main problems they each face are results of actions from different subsystems. For example, Assembly wants to minimize their production costs, which fits well with the 'efficiency' mentality of process control. Assembly, however, continually fights its undercapacity to meet demand, resulting in long lead times, which is a result of actions taken by Marketing and Finance.

From the second perspective (supplier and customer relationships), many of the subsystems have different perceptions of the same supplier and client relationships. For example, Marketing perceives that, as a supplier, they provide Assembly with orders and that, as a client, late deliveries from Assembly affect their ability to sell more orders. On the other hand, the Manufacturing group perceives that they have no

Table 4.5 Stakeholder relationship assessment for Mint case study.

	Perception of their supplier and client relationship with these groups				
	Marketing	Manufacturing	Assembly	Engineering	Customer Service
Marketing	O: Sell more units P: Decreasing demand	S: None C: None SR: Product quality	S: Gives orders C: Arrears affect demand SR: Orders in process, Customer Base	S: None C: Can only sell catalog SR: Product offering	S: None C: None SR: Customer base
Manufacturing	S: None C: They sell more than we can produce SR: Product quality	O: Minimum production costs P: Undercapacity with long lead time	S: Deliver parts C: Receive part orders, bad relationship SR: Expedited orders, Product quality	S: None C: Receive part specifications SR: Technical Specifications	S: Deliver parts C: Receive part orders SR: Specifications, Product information
Assembly	S: None C: They sell more than we can produce SR: Orders in process, Customer Base	S: Order parts C: Receive parts SR: Expedited orders, Product quality	O: Minimize production costs P: Undercapacity with long lead time	S: Send specification problems C: Receive part specifications SR: Specifications	S: None C: Do some rework SR: Installed base
Engineering	S: Give catalog C: None SR: Product offering	S: Give specifications C: None SR: Specifications	S: Give specifications C: None SR: Specifications	O: Best designs P: Rework problem specifications	S: None C: None SR: Product information
Customer Service	S: Leads on new sales C: Maintenance contract	S: Order parts C: Receive parts SR: Specifications, Product information	S: Send rework C: None SR: Installed base	S: None C: None SR: Product information	O: Sell more maintenance and minimize costs P: Decreasing demand

Key: O = Objective, P = Problem, S = Supplier, C = Client, SR = Shared Resource supplier relationship with Marketing, and that, as a client, they receive more orders from Marketing than they can deliver on time.

From the third perspective (comparing the two interpretations), this misalignment ensures that there are probably very weak communication channels between Marketing and Assembly, even though their relationship directly affects at least one key resource *—customer base*.

From these case studies, it is clear that often the misperception between the perspectives of two groups is caused by misunderstandings of the Enabling Resources that each group uses to affect the shared Value-Driving Resources.[9]

PERFORMANCE INDICATORS[10]

QualMaps also provide predictive insight into system performance. 'Lagging' or historical performance indicators show how the system performed in the past (e.g., the odometer reading indicates how many kilometers the car has traveled). 'Leading' or predictive performance indicators show how the system is performing and probably will perform in the near future (e.g., oil temperature is a predictive measure of possible motor failure). Performance indicators should provide the outer limits of an 'opportunity envelope' within which managers and employees can search for opportunities that optimize the behavior of variables they control and affect, within well understood and accepted guidelines.

For example, in the Mint case study, *orders* can be a predictive indicator of the *work load in assembly*. Leaders should focus strong efforts on determining which leading indicators best indicate future system health and the organization's ability to achieve its global Goal. Identifying these leading indicators provides the leaders with measures that cross-functional groups can use to measure system-wide health. These measures should be formalized in the data-sharing systems among departments to encourage proactive management of shared resources.[11]

Performance indicators provide a means of integrating the understanding of the global and local behaviors. This improves the overall understanding of the system.

Traditional versus systemic performance measurement

Providing a systemic approach to performance measurement adds various dimensions to traditional systems.[12] It makes the cause–effect linkages explicit and testable. The systemic approach also incorporates qualitative variables, which are difficult to include in traditional value-driver trees. The systemic approach also adds feedback and delays, permitting easier identification and consistent analysis of leading indicators. Linking the whole system together permits managers to state explicitly how their actions influence strategic Enabling and Value-Driving Resources, as well as Stakeholder Goals and the organization's overarching goal.

Performance indicators and Resource Influence and Exposure

The insights gained from the Resource Influence and Exposure Analysis profoundly affect the implications for determining appropriate leading and lagging indicators, as will be demonstrated in the case studies. The performance indicators given to a specific group directly influence the way the people in that group will accumulate and utilize the resources they control.

For example, if an Enabling Resource within a group's control is in Quadrant #1 of the Resource Influence and Exposure Analysis, then changes in its behavior strongly influence the rest of the system. Be careful, however, with the direction that the group will want that resource to go! If for the benefit of the whole system, a resource needs to be managed in a manner counter to the culture of the group that controls it, then this needs to be made explicit. The group in charge of this resource has to do well under the new regime or it will control the resource in ways that are not beneficial to the whole group.

If a group's resource is in Quadrant #4, then it is a result of the actions of many other groups. The group should not be held solely responsible for movement in their resource caused by groups over which they have no control. The usual challenge to management from this analysis is that the functional divides across the organization often cross through a shared resource, causing the groups at either end to push and pull on the same elements to do their jobs. This usually leads to some serious rethinking of parts of the organization's design and incentive structure.

To set up a framework to learn about the impact of using a systemic approach to identifying indicators versus a traditional one, the team compares the two types of indicators and evaluates the need for new individual skills or core competencies that may be required to achieve the results of these systemic indicators.

Dengue case study

For the dengue case study (see Table 4.6), the locally rational, traditional (lagging) performance indicators lead to poor communication between interest groups, stressing management activities that are often ineffective or counterproductive. For example, the patient to doctor ratio is about 10,000:1 in the rural areas where dengue is most prevalent. Since the few doctors available must diagnose and treat a large variety of illnesses, dengue control was reactive at best (dengue symptoms resemble other, less severe illnesses). Therefore, using *sick people* as an epidemic control metric is inappropriate, unless a true epidemic is underway, and by then it would be too late to act either proactively or within budget constraints.

The newly proposed indicators promote incentives that are centered on the high leverage points in the system. Furthermore, the proposed performance indicators suggest a different set of core competencies for management. For example, improving the public's hygiene awareness becomes critical. Comparing the traditional competencies of management with the proposed competencies suggests a significantly different organizational focus. This can initiate dialog concerning whether the organization can function with the new competencies and what it will take to convert to the new strategies.

Mint case study

For the Mint case study (see Table 4.7), the seemingly rational indicators were causing the miscommunication between the departments.

Table 4.6 Performance indicators for dengue case study.

Functional areas	Traditional indicators	Traditional core competencies	Proposed lagging indicators	Proposed leading indicators	Proposed core competencies
Population	Sick people, Dead people	Responsive approach to threats	Positive receptacles	Personal and family hygiene, Municipal and community hygiene, Population at risk	Improvement of general hygiene
Regional Medical Services	Report incidents over time, Medical expenses	Reporting, Controlling costs, First line of attack	Early disease detection, Medical services demand/supply	Susceptible persons, Regional doctors training, Growth rate of reported incidents	Prevent epidemic outbreak, Education, Population health strength
Secretariat of Health	Report incidents over time, Intervention costs	Reporting, Controlling costs, Responsive controls	Mosquito population, Number of positive receptacles	Control program effectiveness, Epidemic outbreak risk, Growth rate of reported incidents	Preventing epidemic outbreaks
Municipal Government	Municipal expenses, Political problems over time	Controlling costs, On-going services	Average level of services to population	General level of hygiene, New community services per year	Fulfilling basic population needs

Table 4.7 Performance Indicators for Mint case study.

Functional areas	Traditional indicators	Traditional core competencies	Proposed lagging indicators	Proposed leading indicators	Proposed core competencies
Sales and Marketing	Sales volume, Sales growth	Sell engines	Sales growth and revenues, Customer satisfaction	Engine order arrears, Targeted engine attributes	Scheduling engine orders, Matching sales to capacity (short-term), Minimizing engine order expediting, Identifying marketing concepts
Assembly	WIP inventory, Unit costs, Arrears	Meeting demands	Assembly unit cost	Assembly productivity gains, Engine order arrears	Scheduling engine orders, Improving productivity, Managing assembly capacity
Engineering	Number of design concepts, Engine design improvements	Quality engine design	Engineering productivity, Customer satisfaction	Design concept effect on customer satisfaction	Translating marketing concepts into engineering designs
Support of Customers	Demand, Costs	Customer support	R&O revenue, R&O unit cost	Spares order forecast accuracy, Customer satisfaction	Scheduling spares orders, Managing installed base
Capital Management	ROI, Cost of Capital, Investment risk	Make money	Financial risk	Overall production capacity utilization	Managing investment risk

The proposed indicators indicate a customer-focused orientation to management, which manifests itself very differently from the current best-design, or engineering, focus. Imagine how the sales force would change their approach if they were measured and paid for not just selling engines, but selling engines that were delivered on time.

The Performance Indicator analysis shows that the incentives that management puts into practice within their corporate designs determine, to a great extent, the behavior of that corporate unit. Furthermore, the ability of the subsystems to work towards achieving the goals of the subsystem is almost predetermined by the corporate design.

STRUCTURAL AND DELAY CHANGES ANALYSIS

The Structural and Delay Changes analysis focuses attention on the what-ifs. The most important link in the causal chain is the cause–effect connection. This tool investigates the effects of adding or removing causal links in the QualMap. Changes are made based on selected hypotheses the team develops around certain causal relationships in the QualMap. As mentioned earlier, 'delays' are another critical piece in the systems thinking jigsaw puzzle. The Structural and Delay Changes analysis shows the effects of circumventing or creating delays, and improves the understanding of how changes to the structure of the QualMap affect the relative influence and exposure of all of the variables in the system.

Dengue case study

For the dengue case study, various dynamics were adversely affected by long delays: (1) medical staff awareness training; (2) medical alert system development; (3) running water installations; and (4) mosquito eradication. Some short delays are also significant, such as the very short time for the mosquito population to grow. Management dialog should center on questions that would help ponder the feasibility and potential impact of circumventing the long delays, and increasing the short delays. Once the management team has considered new links and altered delays, these changes can be implemented in the QualMap and the new QualMap can be reanalyzed with the other tools of the GRASP phase.

Mint case study

For the Mint case study, the Structural and Delay Changes Analysis highlights the inertia-laden structure of the management system. There are significant information delays that inhibit the system from adapting to new situations in time to take advantage of them. For example, the board of directors only determines changes to the *assembly capacity* on an annual basis. For this industry, that turned out to be too long. By responding sluggishly, the company shoots itself in the foot and accelerates its own demise. External suppliers determine *supplier capacity*. Treating these external suppliers poorly during industry downturns makes them risk-averse to sharing capacity investments during upturns. As a result of this phase of the GRASP process, management dialog centered on the understanding of how to improve the management of these critical strategic issues.

The Structural and Delay Changes Analysis shows that the links and delays in the current structure, as expressed in the QualMap, are the assumptions that govern the flow of information and materials in the system. These are design issues, not givens. Management dialog on the feasibility of changing these limiting parameters enhances management understanding of the underlying paradigms and possibilities inherent in the system.

SUMMARY OF INTEGRATIVE PERSPECTIVE

The Integrative perspective brings together managerial design tools for understanding the following:

1   The influence and exposure of each variable in the system.
2   The effects current performance indicators have on the interrelationships among the subsystems.
3   The determination of appropriate performance indicators.

4   How changes in the causal links and structural delays might enhance or hamper achievement of system-wide goals.

The synthesis of these findings provides insight into the managerial job of designing the structures, incentives, and information flows that make up the backbone of the organization, as well as determining systemic performance indicators to monitor its proper functioning. Let us briefly summarize the Integrative perspective for the two case studies.

Dengue case study

For the dengue case study, the Integrative perspective showed that the variables with the most influence and yet relatively easiest to move, over the long term, were variables that attack the key drivers of epidemiological control. The Integrative perspective also showed that changing the behavior of these variables entailed significant delays and structural impediments to achieve them. By refocusing stakeholder efforts around shared Enabling Resources, such as mosquito reproduction, the leaders can decrease the growth rate of the mosquito population, with activities such as educating the people to remove the receptacles where the mosquitoes procreate.

Perhaps most importantly, the Integrative perspective highlighted the need to coordinate the design of epidemiological control initiatives with the multiple interest groups in a manner that focused each group on actions that strengthened the system's ability to attack the disease, and not negatively affect the other groups over time.

Mint case study

For the Mint case study, the key message was one of managerial design and coordination. The current structure carried an entrenched, product-focused, stovepipe paradigm that inhibited the firm from responding to radically new demand during the industry upturn. Fortunately, the most influential variables in this system, those focused on supplier relationships, were enabling variables in which the management team could intervene quickly and directly. Much could be done to remedy this situation, without making major structural changes to the current system.

SUMMARY OF GLOBAL, LOCAL AND INTEGRATIVE

The GRASP Map and Analysis phase of the Managing from Clarity methodology combines the three perspectives (global, local and integrative) of the systems, providing substantial insight into the dynamics, alignment, and leverage of strategic resources in the system under scrutiny.

'End state' assessment

> My colleagues and I have been here for over 30 years and, at the board level, the exercise showed us that we had significantly different views of how all the pieces linked together. This helped us advance significantly towards a more integrated vision.
>
> (A mining company vice president of planning)

The components of the GRASP framework build on the different perspectives developed during the Managing from Clarity methodology. Chapter 3 assessed the 'current state' of leverage in the system, the system's ability to move itself in the desired direction. From the Integrative perspective, leaders can now recommend specific, systemic 'fixes' to the system. This will push the system toward its desired 'end state.'

Enabling Resources focus mostly on the local perspective, as it is at this level where one sees the relatively immediate effects of their actions. Value-Driving Resources focus most on the Local and Integrative perspectives, while understanding the structures of feedback that drive towards the locally rational goals. Stakeholder Goals focus on both the Global and Integrative perspectives, as they explain how the different subsystems feed back and link together, and how to obtain the highest leverage in this interrelated system. Enabling Resources can be used to enhance the system in the desired direction, but the sustainability of that momentum requires the correct design and implementation of Value-Driving Resources and Stakeholder Goals.

Dengue case study

For the dengue case study, the system exhibits a 'shifting the burden with drifting goals' archetype. The essential problem rose from strict budgetary constraints that control the 'investment' resource necessary for preventive-measure resources. In addition, historically much of the epidemic control in Mexico has been reactive – fumigate mosquitoes and eradicate dengue once it was detected. This reactive nature had proven very expensive and inefficient, in terms of lives lost and intervention resources, especially in times of crisis.

For the dengue case study, the Secretary of Health used the Enabling Resources of radio announcements and free TV public announcements to disseminate the message of hygiene and cleaning up refuse rapidly in the most rural areas (see Table 4.8). Understanding

Table 4.8 'End state' assessment for dengue case study.

Global goal: Minimize lives lost and costs

GRASP level	Conflict that causes low leverage	Fix that creates high leverage
Stakeholder Goals	Population and medical services affect detection and mosquito population	Make all interest groups aware of how they affect a part of the detection and mosquito population dynamics
Value-Driving Resources	We pay medical professionals to service as many people as possible, while asking them to spend extra time detecting special cases	Educate and facilitate the medical professional's ability to easily detect special cases, send them to the lab, and report them to the Secretariat of Health
Enabling Resources	We are fighting the mosquitoes directly versus thinking of ways to leverage our ability	Use information technology to facilitate identification, handling and reporting of special cases
	Doctors are testing few patients and reporting few cases because of the extreme extra work required.	Use the radio to publicize the need to clean up the refuse

the dynamics of mosquito population growth, he used Value-Driving Resources to attack the mosquito population before it had a chance to feed back and grow to unmanageable sizes. He continued to authorize fumigation in areas where the epidemic was identified. Understanding how *sick people* can trigger an epidemic, the public health team tried to isolate *sick people* as early as possible. Recognizing that he needed all of the interest groups working together to take advantage of synergies, the Secretary aligned the interest groups around the shared resources, including financial resources.

Mint case study

For the Mint case study, the firm was following a 'Growth and Under-investment' archetype, as evidenced by:

- difficulty in scaling up production to meet increasing market demand;
- customer lack of satisfaction with the manufacturer's deteriorating on-time performance;
- limited capacity and schedule instability;
- a poor relationship with suppliers.

However, the firm wanted to be a strong competitor in an increasingly demanding and competitive market. The divergence in these two points necessitated strategic thinking in the following areas: information visibility throughout the supply chain; and a closer relationship with supplier that included risk sharing.

For the Mint case study, the leaders utilized the actions of hiring more assemblers and trainers to bring on capacity, permitting growth. They used Enabling Resources in supplying better information to sales about realistic delivery times, minimizing future delivery problems (see Table 4.9). Recognizing the limiting feedback mechanisms inherent with growth, the leaders used Value-Driving Resources to grow their ability to assemble, before the scarce resource became limited. They used Value-Driving Resources to justify early development of supplier relationships, so that they too could help the leaders

Table 4.9 'End state' assessment for Mint case study.
Global goal: Maximize profits

GRASP level	Conflict that causes low leverage	Fix that creates high leverage
Stakeholder Goals	Sales puts orders into the process faster than Assembly's capacity to produce the orders, not meeting Sales' delivery promises. Finance wants to wait for increased profits before investing in greater Assembly capacity	What incentives in the different groups would promote better communication between them, affecting management of the enabling resources?
Value-Driving Resources	Sales creates more orders than can be fulfilled on time, frustrating their ability to sell. Assembly focuses on efficient capacity utilization and highly trained technicians, yet is undercapacitized with long delays to bring new technicians up-to-speed. Finance has to provide high returns to investors, but needs to invest heavily and quickly, adding great risk in a cyclical market.	Give incentives to each group commensurate with the behavior their structure needs to generate Each group must expand their perspective of who their clients and suppliers are
Enabling Resources	To increase sales now, Sales promises delivery terms that Assembly cannot meet. To meet delivery terms for critical orders, Assembly expedites those orders. To decrease financial risk of investment in capacity, Finance leans on its suppliers and on internal cost reduction.	Sales needs to provide the client better information of actual delivery and provide the other subsystems with information about competitive delivery needs Assembly needs to design flexibility into its capacity Finance needs to improve its relationship with suppliers and internal customers.

respond to increased demand, through risk-sharing capacity adjustments. Most importantly, in this case, the leaders aligned the actions of the departments around the management of key, shared resources, such as *orders in process.*

CHAPTER LEARNING SUMMARY

In summary, leaders and policy-makers use leverage in systems to manage resources more efficiently and to design sustainability into the strategic organizational resources. Summarizing the learnings from the GRASP phase, the knowledge of the system's resources and interrelationships was captured, and integrated into a single Qual-Map. The QualMap was analyzed, from the global, local, and integrative perspectives, providing the leaders with dialog initiation points.

Reviewing what has been learned so far in the Managing from Clarity process, Chapters 2, 3, and 4 have advanced the fulfillment of the principal objectives of the Managing from Clarity process:

1 *Understanding of the System.* An increased understanding from the global, local and integrative perspectives.
2 *Ability to Communicate the Understanding.* A single, integrated Qual-Map and easy-to-interpret analytical graphical outputs with which to share what has been learned about the system.
3 *Ability to Move the System.* An understanding of where the leverage is hidden in the system.

With this insight into the system, leaders typically ask, 'Can some of these insights be simulated with our organization's actual numbers so we can test how much changes in these relationships impact overall performance?' This moves the analysis from primarily qualitative to quantitative. This leads to Chapter 5, Key Resource Dynamics, which begins by quantifying the relationships around the key resources identified in the QualMap. Once quantified, computer simulation allows the team to see results for these key resources develop over time under different assumptions around specific policy changes, enriching the qualitative understanding discussed in the earlier chapters.

Key Resource Dynamics: 5
Understanding the Drivers of
the Resource Bundles that
Provide Competitive
Advantage

> Developing a dynamic theory that explained how a complex, key resource
> in public health had behaved and was expected to behave gave us great
> insight into how we could intervene to affect the resource's behavior
> over time.
>
> (A client in a governmental health agency)

In the first phase of the Systemic Leverage framework, GRASP Map
and Analysis, the process explored qualitative GRASP mapping
(QualMap) and various analytical tools, with the purpose of quickly
and efficiently doing the following:

- capturing the expert understanding of the system in a closed, connected set of qualitative relationships;
- developing a shared understanding of how different subsystems
  affect each other and the global goal of the system;
- gaining insight into the system behavior;
- exploring the implications of the interaction among subgroups
  that have different incentives and motivations within the system;
- identifying potential leverage points and key resources.

The second phase, Key Resource Dynamics, and the third phase,
Integrated Resource Simulation, focus on understanding quantitative
resource accumulation dynamics mapping and interpretation with

other analytical tools. Once we capture, test, and understand the dynamics around each key resource, we can connect these resources in the Integrated Resource Simulation phase, allowing us to simulate the whole system. This is discussed in detail in Chapter 6. Why should we focus on the dynamics for each resource alone before combining them? Would you assemble a car or a computer before constructing, testing, and understanding the dynamics of each individual part? Exploring and understanding the dynamic complexity surrounding each resource through Key Resource Dynamics analysis accomplish four purposes:

- understanding the dynamics around the key resources in the system;
- distinguishing explicitly the cause and effects of dynamic behavior for these key resources;[1]
- testing our hypotheses about resource behavior through simulation;
- validating the logic for each key resource.

This chapter converts the qualitative understanding of the system into a quantitative understanding.[2] This quantification marries the creative ability of causal thinking implicit in existing mental models with the computational abilities of mathematics and the computer's interactive capacity.[3] The tool of choice is stock-flow modeling, developed within the field of system dynamics, because of its clear, well-developed, intuitive methodology for examining the dynamic complexity of resource accumulation policies.[4] Furthermore, with the assistance of mathematics and computers, stock-flow formulations help identify systemic leverage points in the system.

An additional strength of key resource dynamics mapping is the dynamic of the actual modeling session itself. If you ask ten experts for proposed solutions to a given problem, you will probably receive at least ten opinions, each of which the expert will defend vigorously. This dynamic only leads to further entrenchment of opinions (none agree, wholeheartedly) or unsupported approval (all agree, but will not support it.) However, experience shows that if the ten experts are asked to map out the structure of policies that determine the flow of material and information in the system, there will be little disagreement.[5] Humans are very strong at understanding how things work in terms of direct cause–effect, but not at simulating long chains of indirect relationships. Put another way, humans are good at laying out the structure of relationships in the system, but not at mentally simulating how that structure will behave.

KEY RESOURCE DYNAMICS MODELING

Standing on the shoulders of giants, we introduce the building blocks of the stock-flow modeling language.[6] Recognizing that these founding concepts were established over thirty years ago, the next two chapters examine some of the advances made in the past quarter of a century in their application and analysis.

Stock-flow modeling provides a user-friendly graphical language to facilitate the use of mathematics and simulation in an intuitive manner. The proof of this point is in the K-12 program that Jay W. Forrester instigated, which teaches children from 6–18 years old to think systemically using stock-flow models.[7]

To show you the power of this simple language, let us examine a very straightforward, natural dynamic from the dengue case study using both ordinary differential equations and system dynamics stocks and flows. The dynamic we will model characterizes a simplified mosquito population (m). Female mosquitoes lay eggs every few days ($t_{m,o}$). After a short period of time (t_l), the eggs become larvae and then adult mosquitoes. The adult mosquitoes die of old age after a period of time ($t_{m,d}$). The adult mosquito population is assaulted daily by climatic changes that wipe out a percentage of the population ($e_{m,c}$), as well as by a percentage killed by insecticides ($e_{m,i}$). The larvae population is killed by larvicides ($e_{l,i}$).

We measure stocks in units of things we can accumulate. The water in a bucket. The food in your pantry. The admiration for your spouse. The loyalty of your friends. These items represent the current state of

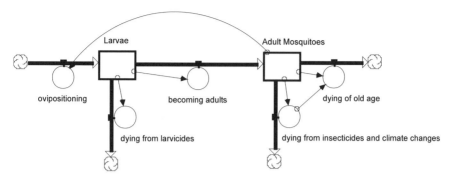

Figure 5.1 Stock flow description of dengue system.

the system, much as a balance sheet does for a business. All stocks have inflows and outflows. Everything has to be accumulated at one time or another, and everything eventually decays.[8]

Flows represent the policies that determine how a resource is accumulated and depleted over time. Through connectors, we use information about the status of relevant resources to decide the rate of flow into or out of a stock. We measure flows in units of things per unit of time. The weekly deposit into your bank account. How much food you ate for lunch. Like income statement items, flows represent activity over a time period.

In the language of system dynamics, we would describe the system graphically, as seen in Figure 5.1.[9] The squares represent 'stocks,' which accumulate resources. The circles on the double-lined arrows represent 'flows,' which build-up or deplete resources.[10] The single-lined arrows represent 'connectors,' which provide information about the source. The cloud at the end of arrow represents 'boundaries,' which indicate that other stocks exist, but they are not relevant to the functioning or understanding of the model.

The system has two resources, larvae and mosquitoes. These resources can be accumulated and depleted over time. The larvae eggs flow into (an inflow rate) the larvae resource stock, and larvae flow out as they become adults or die from larvicides (an outflow rate). The same mechanisms apply to the adult mosquito population. The graphic representation reinforces the important message that there are inflow rates, outflow rates, and stocks of resources in any system.

Table 5.1 Stocks and flows for the Mint case study.

Case Study: Industrial Engine Manufacturer	
Stocks	Units of measure
Engine orders in process	Engines
Flows	
Selling engines	Engines/month
Assembling engines	Engines/month

As a reminder, in the language of simulation, stocks represent resources. Chapter 1 highlighted many characteristics of resources. For example, resources can be tradable or non-tradable which indicates to what extent we can acquire or build an internal competitive advantage. Resources can also be consumable or catalysts, which help management focus on process efficiency issues. Management can also consider their ability to leverage tangible, material goods as well as information for desired ends.

Some examples from the case studies may help clarify the difference between stocks and flows.[11] Table 5.1 lists stocks and flows and their associated units of measure, for the industrial engine manufacturer and Table 5.2 lists them for the dengue case study.

Being able to distinguish between stocks and flows may turn out to be a bit more difficult than it might seem at first. Nevertheless, there is a simple test to determine whether a variable is a stock or a flow. Ask yourself, if the whole system were to stop moving, what would be the value of the variable? If there is still something in the variable, then it is a stock. If it is empty, then it is a flow. An example from the dengue

Table 5.2 Stocks and flows for the dengue case study.

Case Study: Dengue	
Stocks	Units of measure
Adult mosquitoes	Mosquitoes
Flows	
becoming adults	mosquitoes/month
dying from old age	mosquitoes/month
dying from climate changes	mosquitoes/month

case study might help. If the system were to stop instantaneously, would the variable adult mosquitoes contain anything? Yes. So, it is a stock. Would the variable becoming adults contain anything? No. So, it is a flow.[12]

LEVERAGE IN KEY RESOURCE DYNAMICS

This section describes the different diagnostic tools that are used to guide the analysis and testing of the key resources, their dynamics, and associated leverage points. Whereas in the QualMap the focus was on *where* the systemic leverage points were, with the key resource dynamics (KRD) the focus shifts to *how* the leverage points work and *how much* to move them and in what direction. *How* looks at the 'plumbing,' or how things work.[13] The QualMap from the dengue case study stated that the larvae population grew; now the question to answer is how does it really work. *How much* looks at quantifying and testing these relationships. How much of another resource is required to inflow one unit? How many adult mosquitoes are required to inflow one larvae? How does this work? How many workers at what level of productivity are required to produce one engine per time period?

The Mint Group: Sharing Strategic Resources

Have you ever felt as if you worked very hard to manage a resource within your area of responsibility, but the actions of other groups frustrated your efforts? In the case of Mint, a capital equipment designer and assembler, the assembly group was responsible for on-time deliveries. Late delivery heavily penalized Mint, both directly through fines paid to the customer, and indirectly through lost market share. As market demand rose, assembly started to deliver orders later and later. They were frustrated because they did not have the capacity to respond to increased demand and it took too long to bring new workers up to speed on the assembly process.

In the same case, Mint's marketing group was frustrated because they were out there selling their hearts out, taking advantage of the increasing market demand, yet they were getting complaints from the customers, whose orders were arriving late. Marketing started to push on assembly to expedite the orders of their important clients, hoping this would help their sales efforts.

Upper management was at a standstill. They had spent the prior year trying very hard to fix their customer-related problems, yet per-order costs were skyrocketing and orders were increasingly late. As a result, the company was paying stiff penalties of approximately 1 percent of the order cost for every day the deliveries were late. Marketing and Assembly both faced the same problem, but were attacking it as if it were two separate issues, exacerbating their problems.

How does this relate to the resource-based view of the firm? Both groups attempted to manage the same situation from very different perspectives, across functional boundaries that encouraged low communication and low-leverage solutions that intuitively seemed to make sense locally but not systemically.[14] Marketing was paid to sell engines and, given that they were experiencing an upswing in demand, they were being very successful at selling more. Assembly, just coming out of a long stretch of cost reduction, was very successful at being efficient at lower levels of demand than they were currently experiencing. The rate at which Marketing could take advantage of the upswing in demand faster that Assembly could get new facilities up and running. A natural outcome of this situation is a rise in *orders in process*. Imagine the conflict: Marketing is responsible for increasing *orders in process* and Assembly is responsible for decreasing the same resource.

Viewed systemically, Marketing and Assembly share the resource *orders in process*. Each functional area contributes to the number of *orders in process* at any specific time (Marketing puts orders into *orders in process* by selling and Assembly takes orders out by assembling them). Marketing and Assembly influence each other's ability to reach their local goals. When considering issues around a shared resource like *orders in process*, systemic thinking requires the inclusion of both sides of the equation.

Therefore, as shown in the example above, 'shared resources' are those assets for which multiple groups affect the management of its accumulation and maintenance. Usually these groups have different goals and rewards for management of the same resource, and thus their incentives for managing the resource push them to actions that seem logical locally, yet globally they frustrate the efforts of other groups.

Key Resource Dynamics analysis is divided into two sections: the *how* and the *how much*. The *how* section identifies the key resources, their historical and expected behavior, their inflows and outflows, their interrelationships and dynamics, as well as the ability of policies to affect the desired change in these resources. This will be done without quantifying each specific relationship. The *how much* section will quantify, validate, and test different policies through simulation.

IDENTIFYING KEY RESOURCES FROM QUALMAPS

In the initial exploration of the Dialog Initiation Points of the Qual-Map phase, the key dynamics driving the system behavior tended to group around a few key resources. To identify key resources, we begin by identifying the symptoms of the troublesome pathology, then proceed to describe the causal structure that generates that behavior. The analytical framework tests, validates, and educates the team about that structure and its dynamics. From this awareness, patterns emerge, focusing attention on resource policies and structural characteristics. This focus narrows attention to the few dynamics that are believed to explain the majority of the problem. Remember, the exercise started with a focus on the problematic behavior and symptoms, and then quickly sharpened the focus to the resource policies generating the problem – a significant change.

REFERENCE BEHAVIOR PATTERN

As in the GRASP Map and Analysis exercise, the first step is to map out the reference behavior pattern (RBP) for each key resource identified. This puts an intellectual stake in the ground. The team knows the structure, knows how the system behaved before, and has an idea about how it should behave in the future.[15] As in Chapter 2, the RBPs describe two patterns of behavior over time: what occurred historically, and what is desired to happen in the future. In the dengue case study, the advisory board plotted the following RBPs for the key resources identified (see Figure 5.2).

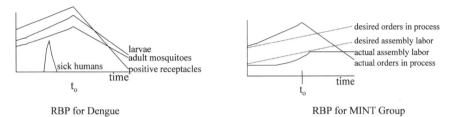

RBP for Dengue   RBP for MINT Group

Figure 5.2 Reference Behavior Patterns for case studies.

In the MINT case study, the management team plotted the following RBPs for the key resources identified (see Figure 5.2). In each case, the desired behavior is significantly different from the current behavior indicating the desire for a powerful shift in behavior across the system at hand — not a trivial matter for any management team.

RESOURCE DYNAMICS

Even before any calculation, the language alone already provides key insights to resource dynamics.[16] An increasing level in a resource does not necessarily mean that the inflow rate increased. It could have resulted from a decrease in the outflow while the inflow remained constant. Though obvious in the language of resources and flows, this insight is not intuitive. While this net-flow analysis is well known in certain applications, like cash flow analysis, net-flow analysis is not often carried over into thinking about an organization's strategic resources and their associated dynamics. Let's see an example.

For example, as we saw earlier, one client we were called in to work with focused all their marketing efforts on capturing new clients. During the past ten years, this policy converted them into a world leader in their field. In the last two years, though, it had not worked so well. What was happening? When we asked them what percentage of their clients were new each year (read: inflow), they had data segmented by factors such as country, user type, and age. When we asked them what percentage of their client base left each year (read: outflow), they knew how many customers they lost to and gained from the competition. When we asked how many customers stopped using anyone's product each year (read: another outflow), they had no idea! The total market's outflow was greater than the inflow, thus the level of the stock was decreasing! Obvious? One would think so, but when it comes to the real world, management usually focuses on inflows when wanting to increase a resource and on outflows when wanting to decrease it. We see this over and over again.

What determines whether the resource is increasing or decreasing? Simply calculate the NET FLOW into the resource, by adding the inflows and subtracting the outflows. In the example above, if the number of customers 'entering market' plus those 'net switching from competition' minus those 'leaving market' is a positive number of customers, then the resource will increase. If the resulting number, or net flow, is negative, then the resource is decreasing.

From the discussion so far, does it seem reasonable to understand the dynamics that are occurring in a 700-variable model? Which resources are dominating the main dynamics, and which resources are not? Where are the leverage points? The level of nonlinear dynamic complexity, even around a single resource, is so complicated that it requires in-depth study to understand. A key learning to this point is that, in order to gain insight into the dynamic behavior of a system, one must first aggregate, THEN look at the detail. Once there is understanding of the pieces, the key resources in our system, then it is appropriate to start to see how they behave when connected together.

To recap, using system dynamics to explore key resource dynamics provides two key lessons to be learnt:

1   Resources increase from a NET increase in flows (inflows minus outflows), not just from increases in inflows.
2   Great insight into the dynamic complexity surrounding key resources is gained at the aggregated level of the system.

GENERIC TEMPLATES

Barry Richmond and his colleagues at High Performance Systems, Inc. have helped pioneer the idea that with just a few basic model structures, one can capture the dynamics of most of the resource dynamics that occur in the real world. The following five basic structures, developed in their book *An Introduction to Systems Thinking*, capture the dynamic behavior that is found in any system:[17]

- compounding
- draining
- production
- co-flow
- stock-adjustment

These very robust yet simple structures greatly facilitate the development and understanding of the rich dynamics around key resources. The following explores how these structures behave over time, the relationship between the flow and the resource, and where these structures are found in our case studies.

Compounding process

With the compounding process, the inflow is a function of the resource being accumulated. This structure generates the compounding, or reinforcing, behavior explored in the reinforcing feedback loop in Chapter 2. A resource affects its own inflow. Multiplying the resource by a multiplier effect creates the inflow into the resource. In the dengue case study, this structure is seen with regard to the adult mosquitoes resource. The inflow of mosquitoes being born every time period is a function of the number of adult mosquitoes in the resource multiplied by the fraction of adult mosquitoes that give birth each time period (see Figure 5.3). If left alone and without limits, the mosquito population will grow at ever increasing (compounding) rates over time.

Draining process

With the draining process, the resource depletes at some rate, which is a function of the resource being drained. This process generates the

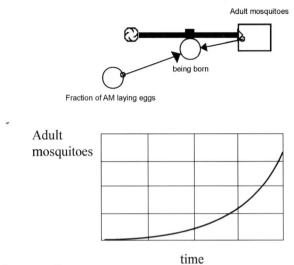

Figure 5.3 Compounding process.
Reproduced by permission of High Performance Systems, Inc.

exponential decay behavior, like the compensating feedback loops in Chapter 2. A resource again affects its own outflow. Multiplying the resource by a multiplier effect creates the outflow from the resource. In the dengue case study, this structure also affects the adult mosquitoes resource. The outflow of mosquitoes dying every time period is a function of the number of adult mosquitoes in the resource multiplied by the fraction of adult mosquitoes that die each time period (see Figure 5.4). If no newborn mosquitoes survive to become adults, the existing population will decay to zero at decreasing rates.

Production process

In the production process, the flow is a function of the productivity and volume of another resource. This structure generates behavior that mimics the resource affecting it. A resource affects another inflow or outflow. Multiplying a resource by a productivity factor for that resource creates the inflow into or outflow from another resource. Since the resource accumulates units of the resource, the productivity factor is measured in units of production per unit of resource

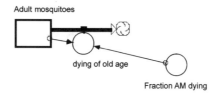

Adult mosquitoes

dying of old age

Fraction AM dying

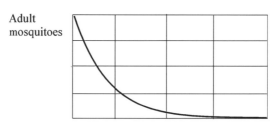

Adult
mosquitoes

Figure 5.4 Draining process.
Reproduced by permission of High Performance Systems, Inc.

per unit of time. In the dengue case study there is an example of this structure. Adult female mosquitoes with dengue had a productivity factor of bites per female mosquito per day affecting the number of people becoming infected every day. Assuming, for this example, that the resource adult female mosquitoes with dengue and the productivity factor remain constant, the number of people becoming infected every day remains constant (see Figure 5.5).

In business, a common example is the flow of goods from company's inventory to the customer installed base. The flow could be *selling*, which we could depict as a production function of the number of salespeople multiplied by the number of units they sell a month.

Conversion flow process

In the conversion flow process, one flow is a function of another flow. This structure generates behavior that mimics the flow affecting it. A flow affects another flow. Multiplying one flow by a conversion factor creates the target flow desired. Since we measure the target flow in units per time period, we measure the conversion factor in units of

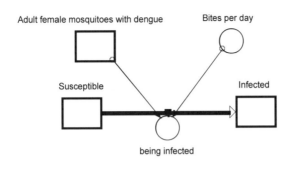

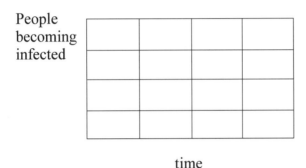

time

Figure 5.5 Production process.
Reproduced by permission of High Performance Systems, Inc.

the resulting flow divided by the units of the originating flow. In the capital equipment manufacturer case study, the flow of equipment being delivered to the customer was converted into the flow of cash being received for those units produced (see Figure 5.6). Assuming, for this example, that the flow being delivered and the conversion factor dollars per unit of equipment remain constant, the flow of cash remains constant.

Stock-adjustment process

The stock-adjustment structure permits adjusting the target resource to a desired value. This structure generates asymptotic behavior like the compensating feedback loops in Chapter 2. A target value and an adjustment fraction affect an inflow or outflow. The target value

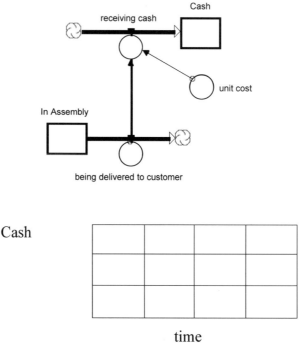

Figure 5.6 Co-flow process.
Reproduced by permission of High Performance Systems, Inc.

is measured in the units of the key resource being adjusted, and the adjustment fraction in percent changed per time period or average time to make the adjustment. Subtracting the actual amount of the resource from the desired amount gives the gap, which is divided by the time it takes to adjust the resource gap, giving the flow into or out of the resource. In the capital equipment manufacturer case study, adjusting the assembly labor capacity is one clear example (see Figure 5.7). The assembly manager decided every few months whether to hire or layoff assembly line workers to meet capacity needs. A negative net hiring rate signifies that more assembly line workers were laid off than hired for that time period.

In summary, we have seen five process structures that represent most of the resource dynamics used in simulation modeling, and with which one can explain the most complex behavior. These are the building blocks of the core of most dynamic models.

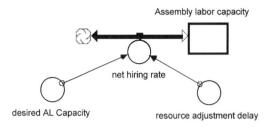

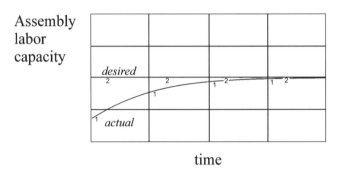

time

Figure 5.7 Stock-adjustment process.
Reproduced by permission of High Performance Systems, Inc.

CONNECTING RESOURCES AND ACCUMULATION DYNAMICS

Once the key resources have been identified and the basic flows around these key resources have been discovered, the next question to ask is, have all of the important flows been identified? Are the key flows inter-related? Often when developing the initial thinking around the key flows (dynamics) that affect a resource, there is a tendency to begin building the model quickly by adding everything that affects the resource. This is closely related to 'correlational thinking' or laundry listing and tends to create great ambiguity in the resource dynamics. We recommend following the simple logic below to help guide the development of strong models quickly. Again, the purpose is to model how the system really works with regard to a particular concern. The following four perspectives structure the identification of the key flows:

1   Principal inflows.
2   Principal outflows.
3   Exhaustive thinking.
4   Level of aggregation.

Principal inflows

To understand which inflows affect the resource in question, assume that the resource, say, engine orders in process, is initially empty. There are no engine orders in process. What process, of the generic templates seen above, would flow into the resource? What process flows engine orders into engine orders in process? Selling. This could be the *production process*, with salespeople selling orders at a certain rate per period (see Figue 5.8).

Another way to see this process is as a *co-flow process*, with the other flow being the number of contracts being sold with a certain number of engine orders per contract (see Figure 5.9). We show both methods of mapping this here to demonstrate that there are multiple ways to express the same idea, depending on the dynamic you are trying to explain.

In the dengue case study, there is a principal inflow to the resource adult mosquitoes (see Figure 5.10). In this case, the *compounding process* represents the inflow of new mosquitoes being born.

Principal outflows

To understand which outflows affect the resource in question, assume

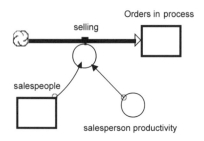

Figure 5.8 Principal inflows.

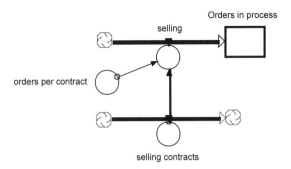

Figure 5.9 Co-flow for MINT case study.

that the resource, staying with engine orders in process, is initially full. There are plenty of engine orders in process. What process, of the generic templates described above, would flow out of the resource? What process flows engine orders out of engine orders in process? Assembling. Representing this outflow with a production process would be appropriate. Assemblers assemble at a certain rate per time period (see Figure 5.11).

In the dengue case study, the *draining process* structure well describes the principal outflow of the adult mosquito resource, dying of old age (see Figure 5.12).

Exhaustive thinking

Once the principal inflows and outflows are defined, there is the question of thoroughness. It is critical to ensure that all significant flows are captured. As said before, a resource can only be affected by inflows and outflows. The number of flows that actually affect most resources is

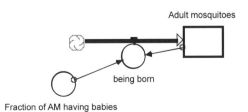

Figure 5.10 Principal inflow for dengue case study.

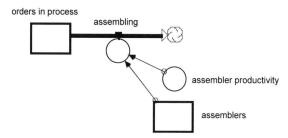

Figure 5.11 Principal outflow for MINT case study.

usually limited, typically two to five. To identify these flows, the question 'What are the only things that one can directly do to cause units to flow in or out of this resource?' is helpful.

For the capital equipment manufacturer's engine orders in process, there are only two flows that directly affect the resource. They come into the process when they are sold, and they leave when they are assembled. In the case of dengue, mosquitoes are born into the adult mosquitoes resource and die of old age out of it. What other processes directly affect the resource? One alternative could be that new adult mosquitoes enter from other areas through travel, which would be represented as another inflow. However, when questioning experts about this, it was determined that the adult mosquitoes do not typically travel out of the large region considered in a way that materially affects this study. In another example, other outflows for killing mosquitoes directly affect the adult mosquitoes resource. As such, man-made interventions such as larvicides and fumigation were added. Adult mosquitoes also die from climatic changes (see Figure 5.13).

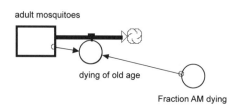

Figure 5.12 Draining process for dengue case study.

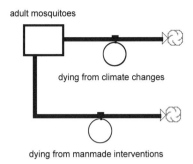

Figure 5.13 Exhaustive outflows for dengue case study.

Aggregating or disaggregating

When thinking about inflows and outflows, it is important to consider the possibility of aggregating various flows into a single flow or disaggregating one into more flows. To decide how far to aggregate or disaggregate, we suggest the following two rules. First, keep the model as simple as possible. If you can aggregate, and the story makes sense, then aggregate. Second, group similar dynamics together. If the adult mosquitoes outflow, *dying from larvicides*, is calculated in the same way as the outflow, *dying from fumigation*, and it makes sense to the story, then we can aggregate them into an outflow, *dying from man-made interventions*. If the dynamics explaining the adult mosquitoes outflow, *dying from old age*, differ from those explaining the outflow, *dying from man-made interventions*, then they should be separated (see Figure 5.13).

'NET EFFECT' RESOURCE STABILITY ANALYSIS

A key concern in management is the ability to move large complex systems; for example, much has been written about the resistance of organizations to change. In other cases, small changes in a policy or action create very large changes in the system's behavior. This next section introduces a simple mathematical tool to help in understanding why systems behave this way.

'Net effect' analysis explains why certain systems gravitate toward a certain equilibrium (stable fixed point), while changing rapidly away from seemingly stable points (unstable fixed points).[18] This technique provides insight into the ability of the net flow (inflows minus outflows) to stabilize or destabilize the behavior of the resource over time, for given values of the key inputs to those flows. For example, in the dengue case study, at what level will the net flow of mosquitoes (being born minus dying) stabilize the number of adult mosquitoes at a specific level or destabilize the resource by growing quickly to another level?

Before applying this analysis to the two case studies, think about why it is relevant to apply it to individual resources. It is relevant when analyzing resource stability at the individual resource level, to understand whether the policies (flows) directly affecting a resource create a stabilizing or destabilizing force around the resource. As at all steps in the analysis, the goal is to understand complexity at the most basic level before proceeding to more complex levels. Once this understanding is achieved, it is time to take it to the level of multiple integrated resources.

Let us refresh the steps of the analysis for key dynamic resources using the case study. Starting with the dengue case study, the first step is to graph the values expected from each inflow and outflow, as the resource increases (see Figure 5.14).

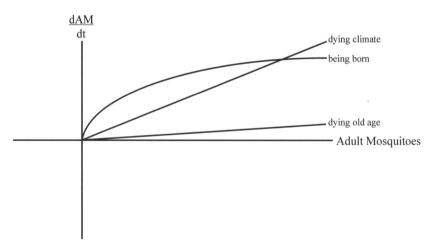

Figure 5.14 Reference behavior pattern for dengue stocks and flows.

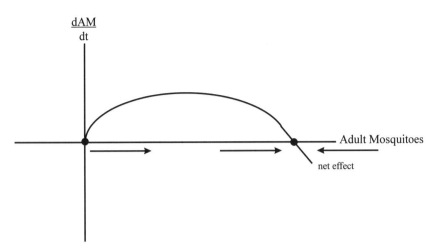

Figure 5.15 Resource stability for dengue case study.

Following the logic of the resource-flow maps above, as there are more adult mosquitoes, more are being born per time period (dAM/dt). At some level, the number of mosquitoes being born starts to level off. The larvae are not able to find enough food to survive.[19] In addition, a high percentage of the adult mosquitoes are dying off due to climate changes every time period (dAM/dt). This value remains constant for any size of the population. Finally, a certain, low percentage of adult mosquitoes are dying of old age every time period (dAM/dt). So far, we have examined the natural processes (flows) within the mosquito environment. What will happen to this population? Calculating the 'net effect' of the above inflows and outflows, by adding the inflows and subtracting the outflows can be seen in Figure 5.15. The population of adult mosquitoes is in equilibrium (does not grow or shrink) at two points – where the net change (dAM/dt) equals zero. The adult mosquito population is fixed at the levels represented by the black dots (see Figure 5.15).

This analysis also shows us something about the stability of these fixed points.[20] At the left dot (fixed point), any small change from that point will result in the resource 'exploding' away from it – so it is an unstable fixed point. This is intuitive; once there are a few mosquitoes, they will tend to procreate very quickly. For the right dot (fixed point) in the figure above, any small change will tend to push the adult mosquito population back to the fixed point. This point is where the number of adult mosquitoes being born equals the number dying from old age and climate changes. This also makes sense intuitively; if the population decreases below (increases above) this point, more will be born (die) than die (be born), increasing (decreasing) the population.

From this example, it is clear that the population will stay at zero until a very small amount jump-starts it. It will grow quickly until it reaches the higher equilibrium point. From this perspective, it seems almost impossible to avoid the system from inadvertently jump starting itself. This says that, from a policy perspective, it is imperative to minimize the higher equilibrium point.

What policies affect the higher equilibrium point? Though it is impossible to change the climate or the mosquito's expected life span, policies can be directed at reducing the birth rate. Man-made interventions can also be added to shrink the population. By cleaning up the receptacles in which the mosquitoes lay their larvae and through larvicides, the rate at which they are being born can be lowered. Furthermore, adding an outflow 'dying from fumigation,' brings the net effect down even further. Both effects are presented in italics in Figure 5.16.

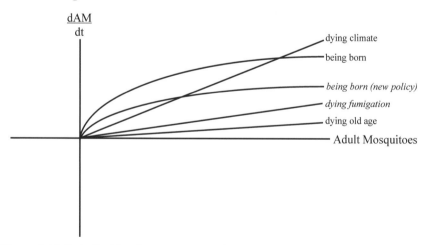

Figure 5.16 Net effect for dengue case study.

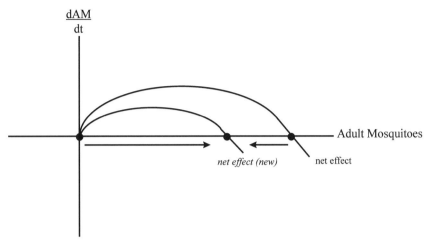

Figure 5.17 Changing stability point for dengue case study.

In Figure 5.17 the net effect has moved the new equilibrium point (stable fixed point) to the left. This example demonstrates the logic to follow to provide four insights:

1   The system will tend to seek equilibrium.
2   As long as the net effect is positive, the system will grow.
3   There will always be a point where the net effect is no longer positive, so it is critical to search for that point.
4   Understanding where the intervention points are in the system can often change the points at which the system reaches equilibrium, thus improving the system.

Testing the policy improvements in this manner sets the stage to evaluate the trade-off costs of different policies – those policies that provide higher, sustainable leverage. Let us look at the same analysis for the capital equipment manufacturer case study.

The resource-flow logic for the capital equipment manufacturer says that marketing is selling (inflow) the number of engine orders corresponding to their market share, for all levels of the resource engine orders in process, until the resource reaches a level where they delivered late to the customer, decreasing the market share. Assembly is

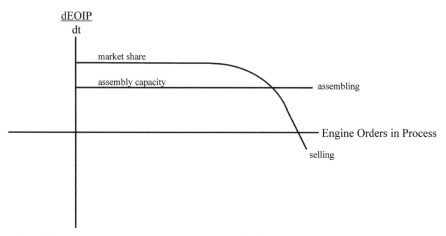

Figure 5.18 Reference behavior patterns for MINT case study.

assembling these orders (outflow) at a constant rate equal to the assembly capacity (see Figure 5.18).

Calculating the net effect of the inflow and outflow (selling minus assembling) produces Figure 5.19. This shows the system will tend to stabilize the number of engine orders in process, where the selling rate meets the assembly capacity, because of the delivery delay inherent in this relationship. Unfortunately, though seemingly obvious, this equilibrium point represents, in this case, a lower level of market share than the desired. Furthermore, the system will tend to push

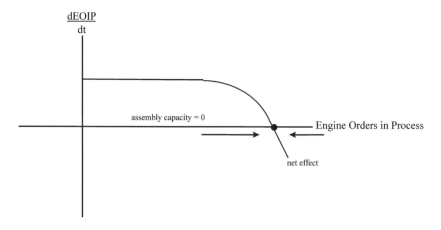

Figure 5.19 Resource stability for MINT case study.

marketing to sell more and more, until they reach this equilibrium point. They will tend to oversell until they can no longer deliver on time. As with the dengue case study, management can test the trade-offs in intervention policies required to change this equilibrium point. Less obvious is the insight that increasing assembly capacity shifts the equilibrium point to a lower level of engine orders in process. The resource-flow diagram helps explain this logic more intuitively by showing that for a given level of the resource engine orders in process, a higher outflow of engine orders being assembled results in a faster time delivery, thus satisfying the customers. This eliminates financial penalties and creates capacity to handle upswings in market demand effectively (see Figure 5.19).

In the two case studies, the net effect analysis provides insight into the policies that tend to stabilize or destabilize resource behavior. These tendencies change as intervention policies change. Furthermore, the stabilization inherent in the net effect of the multiple policies can be desirable or undesirable. Thus, it is important to understand the net effect of these resource policies and the parameters for which these policies stabilize or destabilize. Senior executives know that they should know this information, and understand the strategic importance and implications on their decision-making, but often have had no structured way to get at the underlying dynamics.

QUANTIFYING RELATIONSHIPS

Until now, the analysis of the key resource dynamics model has been based solely on the structural equations implied by the resource-flow symbols, the *how* part of the Key Resource Dynamics phase. Now it is time to take the next step, moving from *how* are key variables connected to *how much* do they affect each other. This part of the process focuses on defining the numerical value or best estimate for each variable.

The initial state values for most resource variables are generally known by the business or by experts. This is because these variables are often easily recognized throughout the organization, such as orders in process and adult mosquitoes. These values are input only

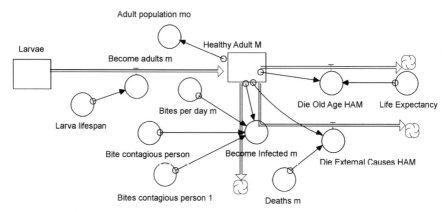

Figure 5.20 Stock/flow model of dengue case study.

once to establish the base case, or initial condition of these resources. For the remainder of the simulation, their value at any future time step will be calculated by the net rate of the flows coming in minus the flows going out as described in the prior section. This is referred to as an endogenous calculation since it is the result of a calculation of other variables within the model.

As shown in Figure 5.20, the adult mosquito resource is a function of larvae becoming adults and adult mosquitoes dying from old age and external causes. In order to calculate how fast these flows affect the original healthy adult mosquito population, we include data such as *larvae lifespan*, *life expectancy*, *deaths per month*, *bites per day*, and so on. Making these variables explicit not only adds to the richness of the story of *how* healthy adult mosquitoes become infected with dengue, but also *how fast* they become infected. This is where collected data can support the values that need to be assigned to each variable.

When talking about quantifying cause–effect relationships, the goal is to put the hard facts of life as we perceive it to these relationships. How will the flows of materials, ideas, money, people, products, and services interact and play out over a time frame that is relevant to the user's needs? Numerical relationships provide a consistent language to talk about these issues because numbers describe these relationships universally and calculate the effect of these interactions consistently and in the same terms. Therefore, here, numbers are very helpful.

However, when taking numbers to quantify these relationships, it can often get more difficult than it would appear necessary. To think about what kind of numbers to use to help quantify these relationships, one can look at historical data, non-linear graphical functions as seen above and simple algebra to conceptualize the numeric relationships that are to be tested in the simulation lab.

Historical data is familiar. It is readily available and it represents the tracking of the results of key elements that form part of the cause–effect relationships under study. These numbers, such as the number of employees, production rates for a particular year, and number of active clients are all very helpful in establishing the base conditions of these key resources. However, rarely does historical data alone provide all of the quantified information that is to be considered. In fact, the historical data points in high level, high insight simulations rarely represent even half of the relationships to be quantified. This is true because many of the key dynamics are based on qualitative relationships that are currently not being measured. In many cases, for example, organizations have very clear numbers regarding operating expense on training in a given period. Very few, however, have tried to evaluate the impact of this training on the resulting level of productivity.

Though it seems obvious that the relationship is important, metrics around this concept are difficult to determine because it attempts to marry a quantitative resource, *money spent on training*, and a qualitative resource, *applied learning*. How does management know when the additional dollar in training no longer produces a beneficial return? How little training is required to get the most out of the learning?

If it is not possible to get all of the necessary information to quantify these critical relationships from historical data, what else can be done? Often, the most complicated relationships are those where a qualitative variable affects a quantitative variable in a non-linear fashion. As seen above, the impact of spending on incrementally new fumigation technology will be significantly more effective after a given point. However, it also gets significantly more expensive. This relationship is not linear. However, the simulation capacity available today facilitates the return of non-linear relationships back into the analytics of dynamic environments. Using graphical functions is the way to capture these non-linear relationships. Three elements are fundamental to using graphical functions:

- Is the relationship non-linear?
- If so, is there an expert available who can draw the non-linear relationships appropriately?
- What range of output is most relevant for each level of input in this relationship?

An example of quantifying qualitative variables is seen in the dengue case, by capturing the impact of more effective fumigation technology on total costs, it is impossible to calculate all possibilities. A graphical function can be used to establish the relationships the experts know to

Fumigation effect cost%   Fumigation effect

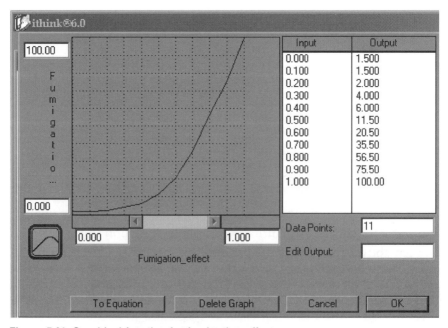

Figure 5.21 Graphical function for fumigation effect.

be true (see Figure 5.21). In this case, the most effective technology was much more expensive than the current practice used yet the range was non-linear, indicating an exponential cost increment for every notch up on the technology ladder.

This graph captures the non-linear relationship between fumigation effectiveness and fumigation cost as a percentage of the budget. Each incremental step in fumigation effectiveness through better technology is represented as a higher percentage of the total budget available for combating dengue. As the technology reaches 100% effectiveness, there is no budget to spend on other fronts. Given that 100% effectiveness is operationally impossible, some balance with other approaches must be considered.

It is most important to note here that the ability to include non-linear relationships between variables provides great flexibility in conceptualizing very difficult issues and incorporating them in the model for analysis. It also allows the developers to capture dynamics around key resources that more closely resemble how things truly work across a range of possibilities that traditional methods cannot.

Historical data and graphical functions allow the user to incorporate a tremendous amount of complex information into the simulation setting. There are times, however, when the relationships do not have historic data, are not non-linear but express discontinuities and potential shocks that may affect our environment over the time frame of the simulation. For example, in working with a utility company facing deregulation in their main regions of operation, certain legislation was phasing in over time and would have significant ramifications for their business model at each point in time. These discontinuities were captured in the simulation environment using simple algebra and basic mathematical functions. To follow the example one step further, to incorporate a $1 decrease in tariffs six months after the simulation point of origin, Figure 5.22 states the relationship for price per kilowatt-hour.

Figure 5.22 shows how to articulate, using basic algebra, the event being quantified for the simulation. The initial value of the kilowatt-hour is $10. It will make a step change downward by $1, in six

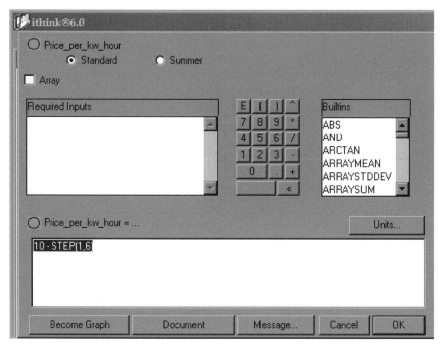

Figure 5.22 Relationship for price per kW hour.

months. Simple algebra is also very helpful in defining conditions under which certain values may be triggered or withheld from the simulation.

The simulation software available today makes it very easy to trigger and withhold values from a simulation. Say, for example, a policy stated the intention to pay out a dividend of 2% if net earnings is less than 100 and 4% if net earnings is greater than 100. Figure 5.23 captures the structure of this idea.

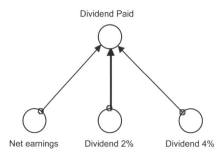

Figure 5.23 Triggering and withholding values from simulation.

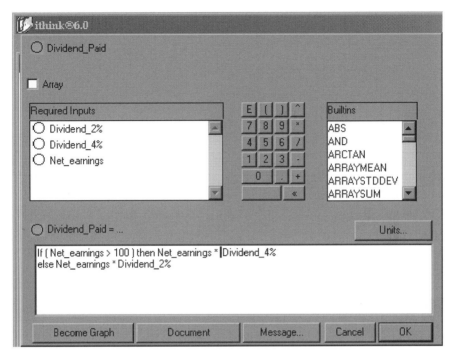

Figure 5.24 Functional definition for if-then statement.

The calculation for determining what dividend is paid will be a result of the net earnings that is a result of everything else the firm is doing over time. Using basic algebra, the formulation for this decision rule is shown in Figure 5.24.

Of course, this relationship is linked to other key pieces of the simulation. The Dividend Paid would deplete a stock of cash that would then limit the flow of reinvestment into the firm that may affect the ability of the firm to generate sufficient net earnings to pay out at 4% the following year.

There are many other built-in functions in these software packages that allow the user to include a very wide range of possibilities for conceptualizing complex relationships. By using historical data, graphical functions and simple algebra, the user can build a robust understanding of the dynamics around the key resources that drive their concerns.

Developing key resource dynamics becomes more complicated as the user addresses multiple resources within the organization concurrently. Capturing the value of each variable and establishing the mathematical relationships among them is the crux of transferring the integrated mental model in the QualMap into the KRD structure that drives the mathematical simulation. The process of making this transition is where users have experienced some of the greatest learning in the entire process. Often users have great detail about the internal processes of the firm but rarely is the data focused on reporting information regarding key strategic resources. As a result of making these mathematical relationships explicit across these resources, we have seen users discard reams of internal reports and restructure their executive information system to report less data that is more critical. Now that these relationships are quantified, it is time to test the understanding of these dynamics through simulation.

SIMULATION

People simulate every day – in their heads. People use mental models to simulate almost everything they do. All plans, down to how a particular meeting will turn out, provoke constant simulation and evaluation of the best way to get things done. Even taking a new route home involves mental simulation before turning the key to the ignition. However, using the same model to perform the simulation rarely happens. Things change. We have memory gaps, changes in emotion, and we think about different things every day. These events can change the basis we use to evaluate the same issues on a different day. As a result, arriving at different decisions from the same set of inputs used on a different day is not uncommon. One of the main reasons for simulating key resources with a computer is to ensure that the same basis is being used to test each new idea of how to manage that resource.

One of the great tendencies of first-time users of mathematical simulation is to immediately engage in moving levers and creating computer runs. Though the temptation is strong, we believe that the last stage of testing a hypothesis is to use computer simulation. The first step is to articulate explicitly the dynamic hypothesis to be tested.

Then it is recommended to refer back to the Key Resource Dynamics structure as the foundation for an in-depth consideration of the expected behavior of the intended actions. This generally leads to intense, often enlightening dialog about the expected outcomes of different pressures on the business' dynamics. It is also suggested to use a 'simulation tracking form' as a means to guide the user's development of a robust dynamic hypothesis to be tested in the simulator. To start, this form should have at least the following information:

- Title of the run – what dynamic hypothesis is being tested.
- Base case numbers for key indicators.
- Description of the actions to be taken and when.
- Description of the expected behavior (we use the RBP technique) for the key variables to be affected.
- Output results for the key indicators – these results can usually be exported directly to a spreadsheet through dynamic data exchange.

The next step involves running the simulation. By this time, the user has a clear mental picture of what to expect from the simulation. Another great temptation is to alter the decisions if the intermediate results do not match the expected ones. Don't do it! In this difference between what was expected and what happened lies the key to unlocking new, deeper understanding of the business dynamics at hand. To flush out these insights, we return to the model structure to trace out the cause–effect drivers that explain the variations.

In discussing the company's business dynamics with the Director of Marketing of a national bank, the underlying structure of business was used to uncover key points in the resource allocation issues such as training, promotion, and new product development. He was struck by his ability to capture such diverse issues and clearly identify how they are linked across the firm. The insight enriched his ability to communicate the logic of his decisions to his colleagues.

THEORY TESTING

Referring back to the RBPs that were discussed at the beginning of this chapter, let us now think about which of the five processes could have created the behavior we described. In the dengue case study, the historical RBPs show that the resources of positive receptacles, larvae, and adult mosquitoes were increasing. As discussed in the section on resource dynamics, this means that the net flow into each resource was increasing. The questions on policy formation become clear. To reduce the accumulation of these resources, two roads are open: either reduce the rate at which these resources accumulate or accelerate the rate at which they decay. Intuition dictates that in order to reduce the number of mosquito larvae and adult mosquitoes, it is more important to be more effective at eradication. In building the simulation structure that drives mosquito growth, the element that most closely represents mosquito reproduction dynamics is the exponential feedback structure.

CHAPTER LEARNING SUMMARY

In summary, the Key Resource Dynamics step focuses the exploration on the question of *how much* these relationships developed earlier in the QualMap in the previous chapters affect each other and overall system performance. To do this, not only are these relationships quantified, but also a structural link is established among them that provides insight into understanding the behavior to expect from these groupings of variables around the key resources. In addition, this chapter described the simplification of almost every system behavior into five basic dynamic structures that increases management's ability to analyze specific dynamics of interest.

To continue the exploration of *how much*, the next step in the process is to integrate the key resources and their associated inflows and outflows into an integrated, multi-resource simulation model. This will be described in detail in Chapter 6 on resource integration.

Resource Integration: Testing the Strategy for Superior Performance

6

The resource integration phase was very insightful for four reasons. First, it asked me to think about things I should know but don't. Second, I learned more about the dynamics of our business in one week of modeling, than in the last two years of 'doing.' Third, a much-easier-to-understand model explained our six-year forecast. Finally, we could actually test the impact of various policies under different scenarios, by adjusting the model ourselves, without assistance from the programmers.

(Mining industry client)

It may be helpful to review the steps covered so far in the process of improving executives' ability to manage dynamic, complex systems using the Managing from Clarity approach. In the initial phase, GRASP Map and Analysis, the GRASP (Goals, Resources, Actions, Structure, and People) framework captured a causal understanding of the system, expressed in terms of key words connected by arrows in a series of closed-loop relationships. The next step used various tools, to analyze the GRASP Map. This phase provided insight about the potential implications and consequences of the causal relationships in the system under study may have on performance over time. Additionally, these tools identified ways to gain significant leverage in moving the system in the desired direction.

In the Key Resource Dynamics phase, the high leverage resources identified in the previous analysis were quantified using available data and expert opinion. Once quantified, this phase focused on exploring the dynamic behavior around these resources, in order to

gain insight into the timing and scale of the often non-linear relationships within the organization. From this perspective, executives could
better identify *how much* investment is required to accumulate and
maintain these high leverage resources over time.

In this next phase of the Managing from Clarity process, Resource
Integration, the integration of key resources enables managers to see
how the resources affect each other over time, in the controlled, safe
environment of simulation. The initial focus is on how to connect
the different key resources into an integrated, simulatable resource
map. Various, straightforward techniques for developing this integrated map will be discussed. This chapter explores new methods
for validating and testing the simulation model. In addition, the
insights gained from the GRASP Map and Analysis phase enlighten
the understanding of the outputs from the simulation model.

CONNECTING THE RESOURCES

This section briefly explains how to connect the key resources and their
associated dynamics, and then discusses at greater length the methods
for interpreting the results generated by the integrated model.

A key principle for connecting resources is to realize that different
resources affect each other across the entire system. This may sound
trivial, but it is not. Most individual managers are extremely knowl-
edgeable about specific pieces that are in or near their sphere of responsibility, but not all their direct and indirect connections with the rest of
the organization.

Chapter 2 explored this principle in the development of the initial
qualitative GRASP Maps (QualMap). That thinking guides the
connection of the quantified key resources developed in Chapter 5.
Chapter 2 also developed the GRASP framework for structuring
QualMaps. This same principle of GRASP applies to the integration
of the quantified resource maps.

These two principles show resource interrelationships and provide a
framework for understanding and representing these interrelationships, in a manner that provides clarity and insight into how to

move the system in the desired direction over time. Due to the inter-related nature of systems, moving them in a different direction from the current course most often requires coordinated, multiple efforts at different leverage points and by different people across the organization.

GRASPing the resource model

As we saw in Chapter 2, the GRASP framework suggests the following structure for an integrated resource model.

Goals: Why does this system exist?
Resources: What resources enable and create value, to achieve the system's goals?
Actions: Where do we intervene to affect these enabling resources?
Structure: How are these goals, resources and actions interrelated?
People: How do the incentives of the people that work in the system affect what they actually do?

Starting with the Goals, we create a converter for the Global Goal (see Figure 6.1). Applying this to the qualitative systemic resource map captured in Chapter 2 for the dengue case, the Global Goal is to minimize morbidity related to dengue. The Global Goal is a function

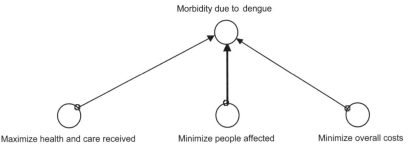

Figure 6.1 Global Goal and Stakeholder Goals for dengue case study.

of achieving the Stakeholder Goals, which in the dengue case represent the goals for the people at risk, the medical community and the government. The Stakeholder Goal for the people at risk is to maximize their health and care received. The medical community wishes to minimize the number of people affected in the most resource-efficient manner. The government wants to provide sufficient services at a minimal overall cost.

Figure 6.2 shows the Enabling Resources and how they connect to the Value-creating Resources to satisfy the multiple Stakeholder Goals. Of course, what matters most is how the different resources create value for each of the stakeholders. This section now explores how the Enabling and Value-Creating Resources create value for the stakeholders.

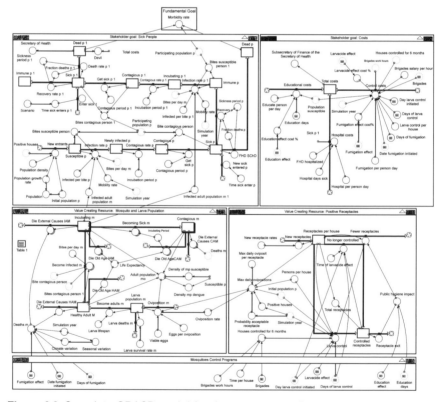

Figure 6.2 Complete GRASP model for dengue case study.

The population at risk wants to stay in good health and, if they do get sick, to maximize the health care they receive. The status of their health is measured in Figure 6.2 by the resource of people that are sick or dead — as long as these resources remain low, the people are in good health. This represents a reverse value creation, or value destruction, function — as the resource increases, it destroys value for the stakeholder. The status of the care the people receive is measured by the resources available per affected person, thus the current health care facilities provide less service as more people become affected. The people use the Enabling Resources of their time to remove the positive receptacles from their homes.

For the medical community, they want to minimize the number of people affected in the most resource-efficient manner. The efficiency and effectiveness of the medical community efforts are measured by their ability to detect the disease and minimize the number of people affected. The medical community also treats the people already infected. The medical community uses the Enabling Resources of money, personnel, technology and physical assets to train doctors to detect the disease, to notify authorities of the disease and to take care of the infected people.

The governmental agencies want to provide sufficient services at a minimal overall cost. The government measures success by the effectiveness of their actions in minimizing the impact of the epidemic, and by minimizing the overall cost of the Enabling Resources. The government uses the Enabling Resources of money, personnel, technology, and physical assets to affect the mosquito population and the hospital services provided.

The next step in the GRASP framework highlights the Actions, as seen in Figure 6.2. For instance, people can remove refuse from their homes. To affect the mosquito population, the government can have brigades distribute larvicides, fumigate, and educate the people to remove the refuse from their homes.

The next step in the GRASP framework, Structure, describes the relationships between the actions, resources, and goals of the model. This structure is already in place, as seen in Figure 6.2.

The previous sections developed the logic, moving causally from the actions to the resources to the goals. This section describes the feedback mechanisms, in order to understand how the satisfaction of the different goals across the organization affects the possibility for future actions. To provide some structure, the initial step is to look for relevant feedback effects at each level, starting with the goals, and then moving to the resources and actions.

Starting with the Global Goal, the following question is important. 'If the Global Goal is (not) satisfied, over time, how will this impact the owner's decision to reinvest resources in the system?' Walking through an example from the dengue case study, Figure 6.2 shows how satisfying the Global Goal of morbidity minimization affects the reinvestment in intervention programs. The government determines the investment of financial resources in the enabling actions. Given very limited financial resources, the government will tend to invest in the enabling resources that most directly control the epidemic in the most inexpensive way. This creates a reactive balancing loop; as long as there is no epidemic, little to no resources are used. Conversely, not satisfying the Global Goal would cause more money to be spent on the resources that enable control of the epidemic – otherwise more and more people will die.

At the next level, we ask the question, 'How would each of the different stakeholders respond if we (do not) satisfy them?' As seen in the dengue case in Figure 6.2, if the people are not healthy, they will cause the government to use more resources, especially in the case of an impending epidemic. Given very limited financial resources, the government will tend to invest in the enabling resources that most directly affect the population's satisfaction in terms of public health, in the most inexpensive way. This creates a balancing loop; as long as the people are healthy, they will be happy and little additional money will probably be spent. Conversely, if people begin to die due to dengue, more money will be spent on the resources that directly influence their perception of control of the epidemic. Though seemingly similar to the Global-Goal-to-Actions balancing feedback of the system 'designers' in the previous paragraph, this feedback focuses on the stakeholders' responses.

At the level of Value-creating Resources (VCR), two questions are asked. 'Does the accumulation and associated dynamics of this specific VCR affect other VCRs?', 'Does this VCR and its inflows and outflows affect Enabling Resources or Actions?' In Figure 6.2, education programs create value by increasing the VCR *public hygiene*, which directly influences the *number of positive receptacles*, another VCR.

For the Enabling Resources, it is important to know, 'Do these Enabling Resources affect the Actions on other Enabling Resources?' In Figure 6.2, an example of this is, to the extent that the education of the public on hygiene and garbage removal is effective, fewer mosquitoes will be born. With fewer mosquitoes, the number of days fumigating and spreading larvicides will be reduced. On the other hand, as money is spent on fumigation and larvicide programs, there is less money for educating the medical community or investing in municipal services.

Finally, for taking specific Actions, the question is 'Do these Actions affect the inflows or outflows of other Enabling Resources?' For example, given limited expert personnel in the medical community, the expertise to combat the epidemic is spread across many other resource requirements, such as training other medical staffers, the population, the brigades, etc.

At this point the initial construction of the feedback structure that interrelates the actions, resources and goals is completed. The final part in the GRASP framework, People, is best described during the exploration of the insights the Managing from Clarity process provides in the global, local and integrative analysis of the QuantMap found in the section below on Identifying Leverage Points.

LEVERAGE IN ADVANCED QUANTMAPS

With the integrated, simulatable resource map complete, the next steps in the process are to do the following:

1   Validate the model.
2   Identify leverage points.

3   Test dynamic hypotheses.
4   Tell dynamic stories.

Much work over the past thirty years has gone into the rigorous development of the tools that enable the modeling team to achieve these four steps. We defer to John Sterman's textbook *Business Dynamics* (2000) for a more detailed explanation of the rigorous methods and tools required. Our purpose here is to clarify the understanding of what the steps are and what tools are available, and then describe how they work by applying them to the case studies. Hopefully, this will provide clarity in why these steps add significant value to the model-building process and model use over time.

Model validation

All models eventually face a strong challenge concerning their validity – how accurately do they reflect the *true* state of how things are? Much work has been done in system dynamics research over the past forty years to validate models. Jay W. Forrester suggested that a model's validity should be based on how well the model served its purpose. Precise models reflect the best understanding of the people involved in the system. Accurate models strive to reflect reality exactly. Though both attributes seem desirable, there is a significant trade-off between resources and value added for precision and accuracy. Generally, it is fairly straightforward to model precisely a person's understanding of reality. It is often far more difficult and costly to accurately model that reality, as too many factors intervene. This brings us back to the purpose of modeling, and thus the criteria for validation. Models are most often used to assist policymaking, thus the focus is on better policy and better understanding of the consequences of the policy over time.

Much work has been done on determining whether a model achieves its purpose, as exemplified by tests developed by Forrester and Senge (1980), Sterman (1987) and Barlas (1989).[1] Sterman's book *Business Dynamics* details the tools and procedures suggested for each test. The tests build confidence in the inputs to the model, the model's structure and assumptions, and the model's outputs. Specifically these proven techniques test the adequacy of the model's boundaries, structure, dimensions, parameters, extreme conditions, method of integration, behavior reproducibility, behavior anomalies, and surprise conditions. These are all valuable tests for confirming that the model precisely captures what is wanted and that the model's findings might be able to be extended to unknown circumstances. These tests also ensure that the underlying structure that drives the model represents the class of issues that are being addressed by the modeling team as opposed to a specific problem at a point in time.

Leverage points

In this section, the purpose is to explain the objective and subjective methods for identifying leverage points within a QuantMap. The objective method applies classical sensitivity analysis to the simulated model. The subjective method applies the GRASP Map analysis to the QuantMap, from the global, local, and integrative perspectives, as shown in Chapter 2.

Objective analysis tends to focus on *how much* changes in quantifiable levels of certain resources impact the behavior of the whole system, while subjective analysis tends to focus on the more qualitative policies and incentives that affect what the owners and managers perceive is happening in the system and what individuals do in the system. Both analyses are required to have an objective understanding of what actions or policies move the system most, in a subjectively created and perceived world.

Leverage from sensitivity analysis
The founding father of system dynamics, Jay Forrester, showed that systems tend to move in a certain direction, and that very few resources have enough impact on the whole system to shift its direction. This insight indicates that for most resources in a system, increases or decreases in their levels will have little impact on the

overall system, and that conversely, for a very few resources, any change in their level will cause great changes in the behavior of the whole system. Sensitivity analysis is a well-tested technique for determining which resources and actions have the most impact on the system overall.

Basically, sensitivity analysis in a system dynamics model inputs different values for a variable, over a range of values, one at a time, seeing how a key resource in the system responds over time, leaving all the other input variables the same. By varying the input from that one variable each time the model is run, you can compare the output to determine if changes in the variable made a difference. Typically the output is the behavior over time of a key resource and informs the user if their policy decisions achieve the desired level for key resources and end values for the global goal or stakeholder goals. This analysis typically proceeds through all of the input variables, determining which variables have the greatest impact on moving the key resource in the desired direction.

All the commonly used system dynamics software packages have a sensitivity analysis capability. As an example, in the dengue case, sensitivity analysis was used to determine which policy had the greatest impact on morbidity due to dengue. While it is obvious that the desire is to minimize the number of adult mosquitoes, which transmit the disease, it is far from clear which action has the most impact on the adult mosquito population. Sensitivity analysis took each of the recommended policies, one by one, to see which one had the most impact on the mosquito population. While larvicides and fumigation had potentially strong effects, their success rates were low (around 20%), thus their killing effect was lower than the growth of the population. The policy that showed the most impact was the removal of positive receptacles – cleaning up the garbage. A small effort in getting the people to understand the importance of cleaning up refuse greatly reduced the number of places adult mosquitoes could lay eggs that would survive to adulthood, thus greatly reducing the inflow of adult mosquitoes. Sensitivity analysis in system dynamics models is easy to do, and provides insight into which variables have the most impact over time.

Subjective leverage from GRASP

The previous section developed an objective process for determining *how much* changes in certain policies affected the global behavior of the system; however organizations are social systems and social systems are messy, political entities. The earlier chapters of this book highlight the importance that local rationales are different from global rationales, and that high leverage comes from aligning them. So, to find actionable leverage points, one must focus on which high leverage actions can the organization actually implement, and what will be the reactions of the other actors in the system. Drawing on the GRASP Map and Analysis tools developed in Chapters 2, 3, and 4, this section walks through the subjective analysis of leverage points, highlighting the local and integrative rationales underlying the integrated resource map.

Global perspective

Starting with the global perspective, different groups perceive and affect the various key resources. Looking at the Mint Group and restating the findings from the global analysis in Chapter 3, the Global Goal analysis shows that the firm exists to maximize profitability for the owners, while the RBPs show the lack of success in achieving this goal. The 'Growth and Underinvestment with Drifting Standards' archetype dominates the global perspective, suggesting the counterintuitive focus on building capacity to serve instead of pushing on sales for revenues. Furthermore, this structure will follow either a sigmoidal or overshoot and collapse behavior over time. At the global level of the system, what picture does this paint?

First, this analysis points out that the management team is unlikely to achieve its desired goals. Second, the organization designed by the management team, either through inheritance or its own doing, will not deliver the sustainable growth goals it has set. Third, the unintended consequences of pushing mostly on maintaining market share, through strong sales campaigns, causes management to create whole new structures in the organization, such as expediting as standard practice, that are only further exacerbating the fundamental problems.

This perspective provides the framework within which we will now explore the local and integrative perspectives. Again, the purpose of the subjective leverage analysis is to determine which high leverage action items are actually actionable within the organization's culture. This global perspective creates the context within which managers will be taking actions that affect the strategic resource accumulation dynamics.

Local perspective

Once again, looking at the Mint Group case and restating the local perspective of the GRASP Map and Analysis analysis, there is evidence that each department's management is trying to design significant changes in their local variables, and that there are inconsistencies between the locally rational goals of the different departments. They are all still in a cost-reduction mode, and just beginning to talk about improved customer maintenance. From a subjective analysis perspective, these represent the local constraints on what the local rationales will permit. This perspective potentially provides a subjective constraint on the high leverage action points identified during the preceding sensitivity analysis. For example, a potentially high leverage action point in the sensitivity analysis is investment in additional assembly capacity. Local rationale analysis in Chapter 3 shows that this investment in the assembly needs to be coordinated with the sales group; however, the sales group currently has no incentive to cooperate. This objective, an apparently high leverage action item, is not actionable under the current structure and incentive scheme. The incentives would have to be changed before it would become a truly high leverage action. Likewise, an objective high leverage action from the sensitivity analysis involves maintaining or increasing sales price! This allows more revenues in the short term to pay for the requisite investment. This policy goes directly against the sales group's incentives to increase sales orders. In summary, the local perspective highlights the subjective constraints on actions from the local perspective.

Integrative perspective

The integrative perspective of the GRASP Map and Analysis examined how to design a set of locally rational actions that supported the globally rational objectives. The subjective analysis provided some high leverage insights into the systemic constraints identified. These focus on the relationships between groups, such as finance's relationships with suppliers and internal customers, as well as information requirements, such as between sales and assembly. By highlighting the incentives that would need to change and the direction that they needed to change, the subjective analysis focused on the subjective leverage provided by aligning perspectives within the system.

In this section on identifying high leverage in QuantMaps, we started off with an objective perspective, running sensitivity analyses, and not the subjective perspective, for two basic reasons. First, it is often instructive to have an idea about what high leverage actions might be taken, before seeing if the system's structure is aligned to permit those actions.[2] Second, at this stage modelers and their clients often want to start playing with the model, to find its hidden leverage points. Following the objective analysis, the subjective analysis examines whether the local rationales will permit effective use of the objective 'high leverage' actions. It offers the model development team a chance to reflect on the logic of the assumptions about these incentives and hold them up for discussion and clarification. At this point, it is often necessary to adjust the incentives and policies in the QuantMap, and rerun the sensitivity analysis, asking the question, 'Under these new incentives, are these still the highest leverage actions?' However, having this clarity on the high leverage points within the system and their potential impact on performance is only a start. This provides the basis for testing dynamic hypotheses about new policy formation.

Testing dynamic hypotheses

By understanding which variables have the greatest impact on key resources throughout the organization, the development team together with the executive team must now design the new policies that will take the organization to the desired direction in the future. There are two logical steps in this part of the process: hypothesis formulation and hypothesis testing.

Hypothesis formulation is based on making explicit arguments for explicit actions on specific variables at specific times over the simulation period. In addition to telling the story of a particular strategy with words in a descriptive exercise, the simulation environment is used to test this dynamic hypothesis before committing the organization's resources and capital. For example, a traditional approach to combating the threat of dengue might have been the following, 'We will continue to fumigate and use larvicides on a regular basis with intense attacks when specific risks are identified. In addition, we will start an educational campaign to educate the public about the importance of garbage removal.' Though clear in intent, this message does not communicate when or by how much these policies will be implemented, nor what types of indicators will be tracking its effectiveness. It is extremely difficult to test this hypothesis.

A dynamic hypothesis of this same issue may be conceived as, 'We will fumigate and use larvicides only before and during the months of greatest mosquito threat, from January to March to preempt them and from May to August to attack them directly. Intense fumigation and larvicide use will be in regions where more than 50 cases of dengue have been reported in the prior month. In three months, we will launch an educational campaign of $5 million in the first year, $3 million in the second year, and $1 million per year thereafter to ensure the rapid and geographically complete awareness program for combating dengue in the highest risk areas.' This dynamic hypothesis can be tested easily in a simulation environment, because of its extreme clarity in how much and when actions are taken.

The second step in this stage, testing the dynamic hypothesis, is then merely a matter of capturing these actions in the simulator at the indicated time. Of course, the purpose of testing dynamic hypotheses is to develop several well-articulated ideas and compare them against a consistent setting in order to evaluate the best series of policies to implement. In each case, the results of the simulation for each dynamic hypothesis should be analyzed using the tools mentioned above.

The insights gained in the process so far need to be communicated effectively to those who may not have been directly involved up to this point. One powerful way to communicate these insights and findings is through dynamic storytelling.

Dynamic storytelling

In the last few years, groundbreaking research has strengthened the modeler's ability to understand and communicate internally consistent, dynamic stories about the system. Known academically as *path loop dominance*, this rigorous technique tells how the system evolves over time, in a structurally consistent fashion.

Based on earlier work in Eigen value analysis by Nathan Forrester and Christian Kampmann, recent techniques developed by Richardson and Mojtahedzadeh analyze feedback in the set of interrelated equations in the QuantMap.[3] The technique measures the impact over time on one key variable of feedback from the multiple feedback loops that affect the key variable. The point is to be able to describe the behavior of the key variable by knowing which feedback loop is dominating its behavior at any given point in time. This is especially important because the feedback loops that dominate the behavior of a key resource shift over time.

For example, from the dengue case study, the resource adult mosquitoes is affected by two principal feedback loops, affecting the number of larvae becoming adults and the number of adult mosquitoes dying. It is important to know whether the population is growing quickly, stabilizing or dying off quickly to determine if a particular policy is truly effective. As we saw in Chapter 5 on key resource dynamics, what we are concerned with is the net flow, as this determines whether the resource is increasing or decreasing. In feedback terms, the net flow is a function of the feedback loops that affect the resource's inflows and outflows. In general terms, the net flow is positive (negative), if the feedback loop for the inflow (outflow) dominates the outflow (inflow). From our example, the number of adult mosquitoes increases (decreases) when the *larvae becoming adults* feedback effect is greater (less) than the *adults dying* feedback effect.

This same phenomenon occurred in the Mint case study with the resource orders in process, which has two principal feedback loops, affecting the number of new orders entering the process and the number of orders being completed. We can apply the same logic as above. Management would like to know whether the number of orders in process is growing quickly, stabilizing or dying off quickly. In this example, the number of orders in process increases (decreases) when the *new orders* feedback effect is greater (less) than the *completing orders* feedback effect.

The mathematical technique of path loop dominance highlights those feedback loops that dominate the behavior of a key resource, at different times, over time.[4] Again, this is important because which factors dominate over time shifts. For example, as a firm is growing, in its infancy, it tends to focus on the inflow of new customers to its customer base. This makes sense, because the number of new customers each time period is a relatively large percentage of the total number of customers. There is a corresponding outflow of customers at all times, but it does not affect the number of customers as strongly as the inflow, because it is a relatively small percentage of a small number, in the beginning. However, once the firm has built up a large customer base, the number of new customers becomes a relatively small percentage of the customer base, while the number of customers leaving becomes a significant percentage, often outgrowing the inflow. This shift in dominance precipitates the firm's need to shift focus from only its inflow to its inflow and its outflow – they have to attract new customers AND keep old ones from leaving.

In summary, path loop dominance allows you to know explicitly what feedback effects are causing the behavior that you are seeing in the key resources over time. This provides great insight into what is happening as well as where to have greater impact over time. This very insightful technique has been fully developed and applied within Mohammed Mojtahedzadeh's work, but has not been integrated into the three commonly used system dynamics software packages.

SECTOR BOUNDARY DIAGRAMS

As one can see, the QuantMaps can become quite large and complicated, as the key resources and associated dynamics are interrelated within the GRASP framework. While the GRASP framework helps make the model straightforward to communicate, the Sector Boundary Diagram is a very effective presentation style that captures the basic model dynamics. As seen in Figure 6.3, the Sector Boundary Diagram highlights the key sectors in the QuantMap, the key resources within each sector, and how the sectors interrelate.

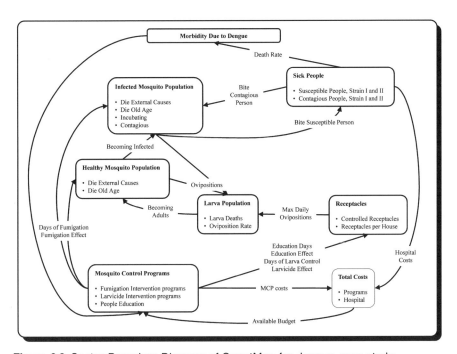

Figure 6.3 Sector Boundary Diagram of QuantMap for dengue case study.

REFERENCES FOR ADVANCED SYSTEM DYNAMICS MODELING

This chapter described how to move the basic modeling skills developed earlier to a more advanced level of model building. While there are excellent books on basic modeling skills, the purpose here is to explore a few straightforward techniques that may be used to gain high leverage insights into the integrated resource model.

Whereas the GRASP framework has been applied to help structure the QuantMap in a clear, communicable fashion, the discussion has not gone into detail about the technical aspects of building integrated models. As promised earlier in this section, it is time to review the best references for advanced system dynamics modeling skills. This model-building discipline requires technical programming skills, thinking systemically, and working with teams. The references are structured in these groups.

Jay Forrester has written various texts and articles on the basic and advanced technical skills required for system dynamics modeling. The insights from Forrester's seminal work and the contributions of many strong thinkers over the past forty years have been captured in a very accessible, well-organized textbook by John Sterman at MIT, *Business Dynamics* (2000). This encyclopedic textbook is a must-read for anyone interested in system dynamics modeling. Peter Senge and Barry Oshry capture the second skill, thinking systemically, very convincingly. Peter Senge's bestseller *The Fifth Discipline* (1990) provides an introduction to systems thinking that has captured the spirit of millions of readers. Barry Oshry's *Seeing Systems* (1996) tells a story, from a sociological perspective, that gives the reader a strong social understanding of systems. HPS's *Introduction to Systems Thinking*, a software manual, is among the finest brief texts for bringing the principles of systems thinking to life in practical professional and personal terms.

The third skill, working in teams, is the focus of Jac Vennix's *Group Model Building* (1996). This explores the methods that have proven most successful in building system dynamics models with groups.

These are among the new classics in advanced model building, and we suggest that you refer to them for what they provide best.

CHAPTER LEARNING SUMMARY

In summary, this chapter provides the ability (1) to feel the power of the insight gained by marrying mental models with the simulator, and (2) to be aware, at a very high level, that different objective and subjective analytical and validation tools greatly enhance the understanding of what drives the system's behavior over time and the effect of policy changes over time.

We have now completed the first three phases of the Managing from Clarity process. Organizations are seen as a set of resources. The QualMap captures the cause–effect relationships among these resources in a causal map. The QualMap is analyzed from the global, local and integrative perspectives. Each tool in the process is simple and intuitive to use and results in a holistic, humanistic view of the organization and the resources it needs to create value over time for its multiple stakeholders. The key resources are quantified in order to better understand the dynamics that drive each one's performance over time. These key resources are then integrated into a complete, simulatable model of the organization that permits simulation of different policy options.

With the integrated model complete, it is possible, and recommended, to test the rigor of the insights gained so far. In other words, will these insights hold in the uncertain future? The next phase of the Managing from Clarity process, Scenario Planning and Strategic Foresight, applies these insights in different future scenarios.

Scenario Planning and Strategic Foresight: Testing the Assumptions Underlying the Strategy

7

> When the authors' colleague, a futurist, presented a client in the tele-communications industry with an oil embargo scenario, the client was incredulous. When the futurist explained the scenario and its significant impact, the client shared, 'This scenario planning exercise significantly jarred my belief that the assumptions underlying our current strategies were right on the button. This made me take the modeling exercise even more seriously.'

In our many conversations with clients regarding scenarios and scenario planning, there is almost always significant confusion right from the start about the nature and purpose of scenarios. The nature of scenarios seems to usually be a financial accounting exercise that the Finance department puts together to project income statement and balance sheet returns under a handful of different conditions that the current market may experience. For example, is the project still viable if we decrease revenues by 25% and increase costs by 25%?

In a world where the movement of capital across national borders was limited and relatively slow by today's standards, this analysis was often insightful. Given today's ability for capital to circle the globe in seconds, some of the foundations of this analysis are less helpful. One of the continuing benefits, however, is that developing the hypotheses on different market conditions usually involves one of the few congenial contacts between the Marketing and Finance areas all year.

In these analyses, the scenario planning exercise focuses on developing an analytical understanding of the impact the different financial returns may have on share price and, hence, market valuation at some point in the near and mid-term. This information is extremely important when considering acquisitions, divestitures, and other investments that depend heavily on external capital needs. In addition, senior executive variable compensation is often linked to this information, and there is an extremely clear personal interest in evaluating the organization's value from this perspective. All of this analysis is important.

However, this analysis views the world based on the current understanding of the immediate world in which the organization competes. This type of thinking about scenarios does not permit the leadership team to evaluate elements on the fringe of today's world that may dramatically affect the organization's ability to survive in the mid to long term. It is not asking the right questions.

STUDIES OF THE FUTURE

When discussing scenarios, decision-makers need to move into the fringe of today's world. If the pace of change is so much faster than it was even ten years ago, then the fringe issues are actually on the near horizon. For example, the existence of the Internet as a business tool has only come into play in the last four or five years.

It is not that the infrastructure was not present; there just were not enough people with the personal computer culture to make a difference commercially. Electronic home banking was available eight years ago and failed in its first attempt, at least from the consumer perspective. With advances in technology, software and user confidence, there is much wider acceptance now. The impact on brick and mortar on investments in the industry is revolutionizing banking. Access to client lists and electronic infrastructure are more relevant than branch networks for many banks today. The result is the natural move towards industry consolidation as the asset intensity shifts from buildings to wires.

To help leaders move out into this terrain of thinking, the emerging field of Studies of the Future adds tremendous support. The focus of this thinking is not to look at the best, worst, and most likely case for certain known financial and market indicators, but rather a deep investigation across a very broad set of outlying issues. This research is called environmental scanning and requires a set of skills that often conflict with traditional, financial analysis.

In order to be useful, the futurist, as they are often called, reaches out beyond the scope of the industry to the fringe of society where trends begin. Petroleum, polymers and pop music all started on the fringe and worked their way into mainstream society and culture, dramatically changing the way we live. Environmental scanning is the active pursuit of knowledge about the fringe, in an effort to establish a hypothesis about which trends will arrive and how we can recognize their approach. Not only is it insightful to foresee which trends will impact tomorrow's world but also essential to identify road signs that will indicate which trend is on the way! Both pieces of information are extremely important.

The difference in this approach from the traditional scenario planning discussed above is clear. Internal strengths and weaknesses of the organization are now tested against threats and opportunities from outside as well as inside the current industry condition. In addition, the focus moves from issues of certainty to issues of uncertainty. Trends are no longer based on financial terms but rather on societal, cultural, technological, political, and economic terms concurrently.

This adds quite a bit of complexity to what once was clear thinking about the future. Given this added complexity, managers again are faced with the tremendous task of integrating this understanding into a practical, useful framework for their analysis. By uniting the strength of systems thinking and system dynamics with strategic foresight, the Managing from Clarity methodology allows leaders to incorporate this new view of scenario thinking into the process of strategic planning.

SCENARIO PLANNING

This section explores what scenario planning is, what the typical process includes, why it is useful, how it can be applied, key caveats to its success, and how system dynamics strengthens it.[1]

What is scenario planning?

Let us go a bit deeper into the content of scenario planning as described above. Scenario planning is a method for developing and exploring alternative futures in uncertain environments and evaluating the robustness of the organization to withstand the impacts of these events. Where conventional planning methods focus on certainty and a single, most probable future, this scenario planning approach uses the uncertainties of the future as a basis for developing stories about the future. These stories are very helpful in describing scenes as they are likely to unfold, even in unlikely ways. This is helpful as a tool to help management identify aspects of these plausible futures as they unfold in real time. For example, from the time Gorbachev, a radical writer in a Soviet think tank, was promoted to his first rank within the government, his career was on the radar screens of Western political analysts. Though one of many unlikely candidates, it was plausible that he could rise to power if popular support for more liberal thinking grew. It turns out that this was the case and the impacts of his career are still being felt.

What is the scenario planning process?

Scenario planning centers around telling robust, internally consistent stories about plausible futures that may affect the organization. The story should be rich enough in detail to serve as a solid basis for envisioning the future. In most circumstances scenario planning will involve the development of several (typically four to five) scenarios. It is particularly worth noting that, rather than dealing with the probable or anticipated future, scenario planning generally focuses upon the boundaries of the plausible future. This takes management's thinking out to the edge of the possible, where significant changes that affect them are born. What is new about this approach is that, as a result, scenario planning generally deals as much with the futures that are not likely to occur as those that are.

The primary steps in scenario planning are:

1   Identify the Focal Issue – what is the heart of the strategic focus of the organization?
2   Identify Key Forces in the Local Environment – what in the organization's immediate world can affect us or do we affect as a result of our actions?
3   Identify Driving Forces – what are the structural and company forces at play that enable and inhibit the organization to compete?
4   Rank by Importance and Uncertainty – when developing robust scenarios, the key elements of the probability of a series of events occurring as well as the likely impact these events will have on the survival of the organization are of most direct strategic importance.
5   Select Scenario Logics – what are the key linkages between what the trends on the fringe may bring and how would they interface with the organization and its industry?
6   Flesh Out the Scenarios – how can we best describe the nature of these linkages and the types of impacts we may notice?
7   Explore the Implications – of these impacts, which ones would most directly affect the long-term viability of the organization?
8   Identify the Leading Indicators – what signs should we expect to see if any particular plausible future begins to unfold over time?
9   Identify the Actors Affected – which stakeholders are affected by the system under the different scenarios, how does this change for different scenarios, and how do they respond?

Why is scenario planning useful?

Most organizations are most ready to respond to the 'probable' futures they see. As such, corporate risk is truly about the firm's ability to respond effectively when unexpected events occur. By dealing with the boundaries of the plausible future, scenario planning helps us to identify and recognize key trends and events that might indicate a departure from the 'probable' future.

Scenario planning also helps us to identify what type of unexpected events may occur and which problems and concerns the firm may face in such a departure from the expected. Exploring the potential impact of broad ranges of trends and events upon the area of concern encourages a richer understanding and mental model for leaders to effectively respond to unexpected change. In addition, the contemplation of extreme conditions is frequently quite effective for getting people to accept the possibility of something different than what they expect.

How can scenario planning be applied?

Scenario planning has historically functioned more as an event than as a mainstream practice, i.e., teams participated in a scenario-planning event to explore alternatives and to learn more about their business once a year. This generally occurs in synch with the early stages of the strategic planning process. In some cases the insights from the scenario process are formally documented and shared across the organization. In many cases the key insights are personal, and often subconscious.

Scenario planning is generally most effective when it is focused upon relatively narrow and clearly defined problems. In many cases, a set of overriding scenarios is developed which serve as the platforms for evaluating a variety of separate problems or concerns over time. One problem with conventional scenario planning is that the different scenarios are based on different assumptions about what is important and how things work – there is no consistent platform for evaluating the problem areas or issues as scenarios change, requiring that each case be evaluated individually from scratch. QualMaps and Quant-Maps provide an explicit statement about the key resources and how they interrelate. This provides an agreed upon map for the scenario planning process and provides a mechanism for quickly evaluating the impact of new scenarios on the problem of interest.

Key caveats to scenario planning

Scenario planning is more difficult in practice than it appears initially. Selecting good logic for the scenarios to be developed is partially an art. The rich experience that senior members of the business community bring as well as young upstarts who question the way things are done can contribute significant substance to the fabric of the scenarios. The difficulty is putting these resources together and focusing their attention on the same range of issues.

Another difficulty is that the scenarios need to be cohesive and internally consistent if they are likely to be of value. A cohesive and internally consistent scenario is one where the linkages among events within the story are well understood, plausible and of sufficient detail to be able to follow the pattern of events in a time frame that management understands. For example, the development of breakthrough products in the pharmaceutical industry takes years, due to the trial testing legislative approval process. On the other hand, the development of breakthrough products in the computer software and hardware industry takes months (18 months is the current breakwater that marks a generation in memory development).

Another risk in the development of robust scenarios is the impulse to look across the entire range of possibilities. Such a broad view of the range of plausible futures takes our eyes off of the driving forces in the local environment that truly impact the firm's ability to survive. Similarly, when identifying the key driving forces in the local environment it is imperative to consider trends and issues across a sufficiently broad horizon to reduce the possibility of casually overlooking or discounting important elements within the scenario. Balancing the scope and depth of the scenario development requires a skillful hand that can manage the diverse needs of developing robust, insightful scenarios that will be useful to management as a planning tool.

Using scenario planning with QualMaps and QuantMaps

There is a strong synergy between scenario planning and system dynamics modeling with QualMaps and QuantMaps. Independently, both require time to fully develop. Of particular importance is that QualMaps and QuantMaps bring structure to the process of evaluating the impact of trends and issues upon the area of interest, greatly enriching as well as accelerating the evaluation process. The use of scenarios to explore the systems model facilitates the identification of relationships within the model that will be strained and may break or require new relationships as a result of the affects of the scenario playing out over time. The primary reasons for blending scenario planning with mapping are the following:

- Scenarios are chosen primarily to 'stress' the relationships in the model to the greatest plausible degree.
- Scenarios and their impact can be characterized by using a visual model (for example, the QualMap) as well as a mathematical model (for example, the QuantMap).
- Scenarios might suggest that new variables should be introduced into the picture to better capture the system's ability to sense and respond to different scenarios.

LEVERAGE IN SCENARIO PLANNING

To add even more clarity to strategic planning, Managing from Clarity uses scenario planning to rigor test the underlying assumptions in the systemic understanding of the management team. How can we get leverage out of the scenario planning process?

As mentioned above, the development of rigorous scenarios focuses on the emergence of a series of plausible events that will affect the organization's ability to survive or reach its goals. One of the key assumptions underlying management's ability to determine the organization's chances for survival is an intimate understanding of the business dynamics that would be most stressed under a given scenario.

This requires not only an understanding of which key business elements would be affected, but also how the rest of the pieces would react in support.

As mentioned before, dynamic simulation tools are designed to explore the effects of external and internal changes in the values of current decision rules within the firm on the dynamics that drive overall performance. Using the scenario logic, three forms of leverage emerge.

First, management can evaluate the potential impacts of different scenarios on their organization's current operating policies. That is, they can run each different group of impacts indicated by each scenario without making a single response to see how the current business would withstand these different events. This provides management with a view to the robustness of the firm as it is being run today when faced with these different challenges.

Second, management can take each scenario, run a base case, and then explore how the leadership team would change their current policies in the face of the new scenario challenges. This exercise provides management with insight into how different people within the group would approach these scenario challenges, given their different mental models of the organization and its environment. Insight is gained not only by exploring and analyzing the potential results on the business but also on how each member of the leadership team envisions the path to survival and success under different conditions. By providing a consistent basis to test these multiple ideas, the simulation adds tremendous strength to the corporate team building process that scenario planning begins.

Finally, using the simulation environment as the backdrop to testing management's ideas, a clear identification of the milestones the team should expect as the next plausible future actually unfolds can be explicitly articulated. This adds strength to strategic foresight for the leadership team by enabling them to communicate to the organization why they are, or will be, experiencing particular stresses.

APPLYING SCENARIO PLANNING TO A SYSTEMIC SIMULATION

The following case studies present applications of the scenario planning process to the simulated models developed in previous chapters. As these applications started during the early 1990s, this section reports how scenario planning was applied to the models and how scenario planning was useful for the Secretary of Health of Mexico and Mint group planning process.

Dengue

For the dengue case, the following depicts the environment in Mexico at the time the project was undertaken. During the early 1990s, the Secretary of Health of Mexico was facing the threat of hemorrhaging dengue becoming an epidemic in the southern part of the country. Several deaths due to hemorrhaging dengue were reported in Guatemala. More cases were being reported monthly. The alarm had been sounded and a potential public health risk was identified.

Politically, Mexico was on very strong footing with the widely regarded presidency of Carlos Salinas. Salinas was regarded as a savvy politician, a charismatic leader and an economic visionary. Economically, the landmark signing of the North American Free Trade Agreement (NAFTA) linked Mexico to an extremely favorable expected economic future of opportunity and stability. There was a sense that the Mexican development model was the right one for all of South America. In addition, Mexico became a focal point for significant inflows of foreign investment capital.

Culturally, there was a sense of privilege of being part of that experiment. Anything seemed possible. The globalization of Mexico and the export of its culture expanded tremendously. A symbol of this may be the tremendous growth in the export of tequila and the perception of tequila as upmarket liquor: a far cry from its perception in the 1980s.

Socially and technologically, the growth in the expatriate community and the introduction of many multinational companies created areas of great opportunity professionally. The often-stated love–hate relationship with the USA softened a bit. Music and fashion from the States penetrated the fiber of Mexican youth more strongly. On the other side of the coin, the distinctions among the social classes in Mexico were not only highlighted but also widened. Some of this increasing separation was, and continues to be, due to the need to be technologically literate, often in English, in order to participate in the NAFTA-driven sectors of the economy where growth is assumed to reside.

This background framed the discussions on the strategic planning against the dengue threat. As discussed earlier, two main points of dialog arose from the Managing from Clarity methodology: the short-term solution of fumigating and using insecticides was not effective for eradication of the threat, but did provide political support from the community by being visibly active. The other point focused on the long-term solution of educating the population to remove the receptacles in which the dengue-carrying mosquitoes breed, to eliminate the risk at its core.

With regard to fumigation and use of insecticides, the assumption of a stable, growing economy led the team to push for the most expensive solutions. The more technologically advanced products and processes would be far more effective than the current ones. This made perfect sense and was seen as socially and politically very important. The scenario planning exercise permitted exploration of these more deeply held assumptions by asking for disconfirming truths – what would make this hypothesis wrong. One of the answers was that there would be some event that would eliminate the access to the necessary funds to implement this advanced technology solution in the short term. This raised questions on the assumptions of the nation's expected political and economic stability borne out of the signing of NAFTA in 1993. One of the goals of NAFTA was to ensure a smooth economic transition that had so often failed in the presidential election process. The 1995 elections had just passed. Nonetheless, the expectations of a growing economy and smooth political transition led the team to embark on a significant attack on the dengue threat, with expensive technology leading the front. The thinking at the time was to provide a powerful frontal attack on dengue wherever it appeared and push for eradication in those areas. A small portion of the limited budget was earmarked for education. The thinking was to let dengue run its course and outrun it before it invaded Mexico in a significant way.

In hindsight, the economic crisis that started in Mexico after the presidential elections in 1994 was obvious. The resulting devaluation and economic shock left many businesses bankrupt, for they had financed their expected growth in dollars, and many investment projects were cancelled. The capital flight also affected the Secretary of Health. The technologically superior products that were the backbone of this part of the strategy became astronomically expensive. Fortunately, the team had a second plan in the event the conditions changed. The scenario planning exercise helped sensitize the team to radically different conditions that in fact did prevail.

The benefit of this exercise to the Secretary of Health and his team was the ability to respond quickly and coherently to these dramatic changes in an effective way. The shift in focus to education as the major thrust permitted the team to effectively address the threat of dengue. In addition, fumigation and use of insecticides continued to be part of the strategy though on a smaller scale. This approach required the Secretary of Health to marshal his forces across a wider base of action, including the media, the press and many individuals, than would have been required for the more expensive, technology-driven approach. The result is what matters, however, and, to date, there has been no hemorrhaging dengue epidemic in Mexico.

The Mint Group

In the case of the Mint Group, demand is cyclical and the experts believe that the cycles turn every seven to ten years. Capital investments are significant and the delays in bringing capacity on line are important, ranging from 18 to 24 months. Before the time of the project engagement, the industry had been suffering a continued contraction. After seven years of a continual downturn in demand, signs of a reversal were showing. In addition, though the company's sales were increasing, their profits were not. Much of the cause in lost margins was due to the fines that were being paid for late deliveries, which also were adversely affecting relationships with important customers. The challenge facing the management team was the following: To take advantage of an upswing in demand will require time and money, should they invest now in increased capacity or fix the short-term service and profitability concerns?

Politically and economically, this country was suffering an economic downturn as well in the early 1990s. By the middle of the decade, the currency was weakening with regard to others and there was an ongoing dispute among the seats of government about the appropriate road to take. Government dialog was alive and, at times, confrontational over the issues of participation in a greater economic union with other nations and over proposals for specific trading agreements kept.

Culturally, competition and free market challenges continued to pressure rules of social conduct. The search for national identity combined with the economic stresses increased the antagonism towards immigrants who were willing to work for less. Within the business, seven years of decline in demand had focused the firm on cost reduction, not on investment in capacity. Fear of job loss reduced the tolerance for risk taking and innovation. As such, the Mint executives had become extremely expert in efficiency and cost management programs. The resurgence in demand came to the attention of senior management when the CFO began to see sales increase and profits decrease. Where had all of this cost control expertise gone?

Socially and technologically, the nation was experiencing higher levels of unemployment than its neighbors, generating a sense of uncertainty and stress at the family level and in business relationships. The search for making ends meet resulted in intense competition for all levels of employment. The search for differentiation in skills also highlighted greater opportunities for those with technological skills over industrial skills, shifting the focus of the nation's best and brightest. Growing capacity at this time would also imply finding or developing skilled key talent in time to support this expanded production machine.

This is the context in which the Mint Group executives discussed their scenario planning issues. The Managing from Clarity methodology, as seen in Chapters 4 and 5, highlighted the fix for the customer service issues and subsequent financial penalties that were being paid. It became clear that it was more profitable to sell a bit less in the rising market and deliver on time than just sell at the pace of market growth. This answered one series of issues but not the long-term issue of adding capacity or not. The scenario planning group had to answer the question of whether or not this was just a rebound or a true reversal in market demand.

To do this, the team again looked for confirming and disproving evidence of true market growth. Confirming this growth was evidence from existing clients who were asking for additional units. However, growth from the existing client base would not warrant investment in new capacity. The team then asked, 'What indications on the frontier of today's understanding would suggest a true increase in demand?'

The industries that used the Mint Group's products in the developed nations were growing, but slowly. The scenario planning approach took the team out of the current understanding of market reality and allowed them to consider game-changing evolutions in the market. Among these was the consideration of the impact a true economic boom in the East and Latin America may have on their industry. Once they started looking outside current boundaries of their market, it became clear that a strong sector of possible growth could emerge from the developing nations over the mid-term not just over the long term.

This realization focused the group's thinking on developing road signs that would indicate the next jump in demand from this sector. Though no immediate investment in additional capacity was recommended at the time, a flexible response initiative was developed to track movement in demand from the frontier markets.

As it turned out, the Mint management team did not have to wait long for the new demand indicators to be recognized. Eighteen months later the Asian market showed signs of sustained growth and the Mint Group invested in its newest facility in a timely manner. The GRASP approach had provided the management team with the necessary strategic clarity to optimize profitability within the existing capacity as demand grew in the short term as well as invest in new capacity at the right time to capture the rising demand.

Learning Interfaces: Communicating the Robust Model

8

We can say that we understand our business model all we want, but when you are interfacing with the learning environment and the indicator is flashing red in your face, telling you that you are messing up, then you begin to realize that maybe you don't understand your business as well as you should. Makes you think.

> (The director of a large utility company, when the authors demonstrated the learning interface to be used during the client's war gaming exercise)

Learning Interfaces (LI) represent all forms of user interfaces developed to enable individuals to interact with a simulator. We think about three types of interfaces that can be developed to cover very different needs. We begin the chapter with background on LIs, from the theoretical and design perspectives. We then explain each of the three LI types in more detail. We finish with a discussion about the evolution and growing applications of business simulation and LIs today.

LEARNING INTERFACES BACKGROUND

Business simulation and executive war gaming are growing rapidly as increasing computer power facilitates the creation of ever more sophisticated simulations. Good simulations facilitate the development of more sophisticated mental models, focus conversations among executive teams, and, as a result, facilitate more effective problem solving. Rather than learning by being told, the participants have an opportunity to learn by doing. By including simulation in the management process, executives can now take advantage of the benefits of double-loop learning on a broader scale within the organization.

DOUBLE-LOOP LEARNING[1]

Double-loop learning provides the individual with the opportunity to test an idea out, see the likely results, modify the idea, and test it again in a safe, laboratory-like setting before putting the idea into action in the organization. This is analogous to the way engineers test memory chips and petroleum pipelines before going into production.

A primary difference between single and double-loop learning involves the openness of the underlying paradigms to inspection and modification. In single-loop learning the individual observes a situation, evaluates its deviation from some desired condition, and makes some adjustment to improve the situation (see Figure 8.1). Based upon the changes in the condition, additional adjustments will be made. In real life, the delay from the moment of an action to

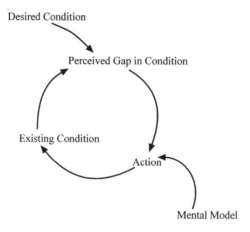

Figure 8.1 Single-loop learning.

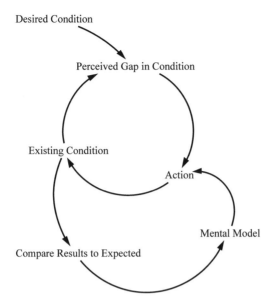

Figure 8.2 Double-loop learning.

the resulting change in the condition is often substantial. This delay makes it very difficult to carefully evaluate the action and the resulting change in the condition. In addition, other factors may change, making interpretation difficult.

In double loop learning, the process of reflection is included, using simulation (see Figure 8.2). Simulation allows the user to compress time so that adjustments can be evaluated in concert with the resulting change in the existing situation. If the existing condition changes in an unexpected way from a particular action, the mental model may be questioned. Experimentation and learning may occur.

Delays and 'noise' combine to frustrate double-loop learning in real life. Simulations and games provide advantageous environments for double loop learning by allowing them to see the effects of reducing delays between adjustment and results. In addition, simulation focuses on the elements that truly drive the key variables of concern and allows the users to isolate the 'noise,' or exogenous factors, and treat them independently.

What are Learning Interfaces?

One of the most effective forms of learning has always been learning by doing. However, in complex systems, time, delays, and ambiguous consequences from previous actions combine to impede learning. It is hard to associate specific outcomes from specific actions when so much is going on at the same time. Effective learning in complex environments can be accelerated by creating an environment where the effects of actions in a system can proceed quickly, the results studied, and hypotheses concerning how the system works can be tested repeatedly. Such is the environment that pilots use in flight simulators. LIs present a flight-simulator interface to the mathematical simulator and can communicate systems understanding through various means.

Why are Learning Interfaces useful?

These simulators present pilots in training with real-life possibilities in a controlled environment in order to test, modify and eventually hard code into the pilot the ability to consistently assess a new situation and act accordingly across a broad range of possibilities. The same approach can be used by managers to explore their complex decision environments by testing their skills and understanding in LIs based on models that simulate their businesses. This invokes the double-loop learning discussed above.

How can Learning Interfaces be applied?

Because LIs compress time and allow the user to 'live the future vicariously,' LIs can be valuable in a variety of situations, from hypothesis testing and training to war gaming and scenario planning.

Executive hypothesis testing

Executives all test their hypotheses in their heads before implementing them. This is not the question. The issue is that each executive affected by the decision also tests the impacts on their part of the business … in their head. As they report to their staff what must be done, each staff member simulates the effect on their part of the business ... in their head. What is the probability that all of these key players are using the same structural business model to evaluate the impacts on them of the leadership team's action? Given that each member is only responsible for a piece of the business, what is the likelihood that they can, or will, consider the effects of what they do on other members of the firm? Are they rewarded for doing this?

As you can see, executive hypothesis testing is not a trivial matter at all. In our experience, the lack of a shared business model across the leadership team leads to the majority of internal conflict within the organization. LIs offer the ability to develop a common business model for the executive team and their reports, to explore their ideas and the potential impacts against a consistent framework. So when the question is asked, 'What will we do to get from here to there and in what time frame?,' the dialog will center on the impacts on the business model and less on the power of persuasion from strong personalities and pure intuition.

Executive and operations training

The LI can also be used to inform new arrivals and enrich existing executives' conceptual understanding of the nature of cause and effect within the organization and its dynamic impacts on performance over time.

> It is so clear where all of the pieces fit together when seen this way. We should consider using this tool to train all of our new employees in how we think about our business. It is all here and they can identify where they sit within the organization and where they fit within the greater whole.
>
> (Director of Operations of a national Mexican insurance company)

In addition, the logic behind all major initiatives and programs can be explicitly described in terms of the business model. This way, all members of the firm can understand why the leadership team is doing what it is doing.

War gaming

LIs support the concept of war gaming by providing insight into how the competition may respond to new conditions as well as how different teams within the organization handle the same challenges. We will discuss this idea in more detail below.

Scenario planning

The LIs also help the user explore how the firm will respond under different plausible futures. We discussed scenario planning in detail in Chapter 7.

DESIGN ISSUES FOR LEARNING INTERFACES

Much ado is being made about LIs. They are called executive flight simulators, dashboards, learning laboratories, learning environments, and microworlds. Are these all the same thing with just different names or is there a difference? To clarify our thinking, we distinguish three levels of learning interfaces, based on the level of interactive learning in the simulated environment. The levels are:

1   dashboards
2   laboratories
3   learning environments.

To compare and contrast the three levels, this section discusses how they each focus on interactive learning, their key benefits, their limitations, and their intended end user.

Dashboards

Dashboards are the simplest. A dashboard focuses on the ability to make key decisions and see key resource outputs. The design challenges facing the developers is one of ensuring that the user has access to the key levers for decisions and outputs for the variables they directly affect. There is no additional consideration given to the exploration of any relationship in particular. For example, a dashboard for the equipment manufacturer may include a demand lever and, on the same screen an output graph of total units sold per month. On another graph, we may see new orders per month and backlog. The causality is direct and clear.

The learning derived from the dashboard interface depends fully on the user's ability to interpret the results in a dynamic setting. This means the user brings the ability to understand the underlying causality in the model structure either implicitly through the model behavior or through knowledge of the model's stocks and flows.

It would seem apparent that any businessperson would intimately understand these issues, especially in his or her own company. However, as we mentioned before, given that there is far too much detail in the reality of the business for any individual to capture everything, each person aggregates the world around them into pieces they can understand. Once again, it is very unlikely that all members of the firm aggregate the world around them in exactly the same fashion. As a result, each user brings their own set of assumptions and aggregations to the table when they use the simulator. Therefore, it is very likely that the same results will be interpreted differently across the management team.

The dashboard approach is most often used when the model developers are the target users. In this way, the assumptions of all of the developers are known to each other and, as a result, the guide to interpreting the results is the same.

Learning laboratories

Learning laboratories (LL) take the dashboard to the next level of interactive learning, providing feedback to the user DURING the simulation. In the LL, the development team thinks about the key levers and outputs to provide for the user, and the key assumptions being tested in the model. This increases the design challenges. The developers now must indicate the path of learning that the simulation is trying to transmit in the design of the interface. In our experience, the structure of the LL is different from the dashboard in several ways.

First, in the LL, there is a clear intention not only to show the causality of the decision points and their outputs but also the causality among the outputs. For example, we may add monthly financial fines to the backlog graph to show the linkage between operations and finance. In this way, the developers help the user make the connection between backlog and financial fines, which is not always obvious.

In addition, the simulation software available today allows for great flexibility in showing the firm's policies regarding fluctuations in results. Whereas in the dashboard the outputs merely show the results, in the LL the developers can input messages if the figures move outside of a pre-determined range. For example, management may agree that the average number of backorders is two months' worth of sales, due to the assembly time. With management's view of the policy, the developer can indicate an acceptable range of one to two months' worth of backlog and not stop the simulation. If the backorder level gets below one month or above two months, however, a warning message may appear advising the user that he has fallen out of the acceptable operating range for backorders, based on his decisions during the simulation. Other messages may be included to inform the user to watch out for certain trends as other key variables, such as fine paid or units sold move out of their acceptable ranges. There is tremendous flexibility available to the management team in supporting the development teams design of the LL interface.

The result is a learning experience where the user is guided away from extremes and stopped if the results fall out of the acceptable range. This provides the user with a sense of reality, as poor results will stop the simulation much in the same way that the shareholders may change management for the same reasons.

Learning Environments

Learning Environments (LE) enhance the interactive learning experience to become an autodidactic coaching tool. In both the dashboards and the LLs, the underlying business model represents the firm's best thinking about how the business actually runs from the multiple perspectives mentioned earlier. The focus is on developing a model that reflects the business as it is. The design issues do not intend to change any of the causality within the business but rather explore it in more or less detail.

In the LE, the issues of design are pushed to the limit. From its inception, the conceptualization of the LE is different. The focus is on addressing key learnings that the executive team wants to transmit and the model is developed to support those learnings. As such, the assumptions of the underlying model may change to ensure that the simulation results drive the user to make a pre-determined series of decisions in order to highlight a particular learning. For example, High Performance Systems, Inc and Harvard Business School Publishing released an interactive educational CD called 'Balancing the Corporate Scorecard.' The purpose is to explore the topic of the Balanced Scorecard management approach presented in Robert Kaplan and David Norton's leading book, *The Balanced Scorecard: Translating Strategy into Action* (1996).

The interactive simulation puts the reader in charge of a fictitious company and compares the ability to run the firm with purely traditional financial data and then with the elements of the Balanced Scorecard. The underlying simulation was built with the sole purpose of describing and exploring the theory and use of the principles of the Balanced Scorecard. Graphics, text, video and audio platforms were woven into the fabric of the simulation so that by the end of the two-hour experience, the user had acquired not only the information regarding the basic principles of the scorecard but also a hands-on experience in developing one and putting it to work – all in two hours. This is the power of creating a learning environment – the experience is fast and the learning is very directed.

As such, the design issues are much more complex than for dashboards and LLs. In LEs, the entire learning experience needs to be mapped out before the model structure is even considered. When building the model, the variable parameters are calibrated to

Table 8.1 Attributes of the three types of Learning Interfaces.

	Dashboard	Learning Lab	Learning Environment
Focus on interactive learning	Flight simulator interface highlights key behaviors and test assumptions on an iterative basis.	Flight simulator interface focuses on generating discussion around key assumptions and sharing across executives well versed in the business issues being explored and hypotheses being tested.	Flight simulator teaches insights around key dynamics affecting key resources. Focus is on communicating non-intuitive implications of seemingly clear actions across a broad range of users. Learning by doing, followed by a debrief that is incorporated into the design of the extremely interactive experience.
Benefits	Excellent for practitioners who are skilled at changing the simulation outputs as needed. Very flexible.	Focuses management team on critical dynamics generating the situation in question. Conversation centers on objective understanding and implications of causality, feedback and delays in strategic context.	Extremely powerful in communicating complex dynamics across a broad range of potential users.
Limitations	No guidance in interpreting the simulation results. Communicating the logic of the results is not clear since no guidance is given as to how the underlying relationships drive results.	Questions may arise as to the source and quantification of the cause–effect relationships. Effective use requires appropriate selection of levers and output metrics and strong facilitation skills. The learning curve is steeper than with some other analytical tools (but well worth it!).	The most difficult to build – requires a clear understanding of the learning to be presented as part of the model conceptualization and design. Changes to the model are more difficult and adaptation for new purposes is challenging.
Intended end user	Modeling team	Executives and managers familiar with the issues and general business/ organizational conditions affecting issue at hand	Wide range of users within and outside of the organization.

deliver the desired results for the learning experience and not just to track a historic data set. LEs tend to be costly and directed to a mass audience, either in the open market or within large companies who use this medium to support the transmission of new corporate initiatives.

As summarized in Table 8.1, this section has described how each type of learning interface focuses on interactive learning, their key benefits, their limitations, and their intended end user.

How to select the appropriate type of Learning Interface

When thinking about the different types of simulator interfaces, a key issue to deal with is, 'which best suits the group's needs for interfacing with the simulator?' To help us address this question we use the following guiding thoughts:

1 Who is the audience for the Learning Interface?
2 What are the key learnings to be shared in this Learning Interface?
3 What variables in the model communicate this learning?
4 What variables fall within the control of the audience?
5 Should other variables not within their control be included?
6 What variables in the model represent the performance indicators for the audience?
7 For what variables should the audience be responsible?
8 To gain a systems perspective, what performance metrics from other groups should be shared with the audience?
9 Are all the variables defined above represented in the model? Should they be?
10 Which gauge tools (gauge, X-Y graph, time plot, bar graphs, line graphs, array graphs) best communicate the behavior of the variables included?

Once these issues are clear, the decision of which type of interface to build becomes obvious. For most business settings, the dashboard or Learning Lab approach are the most used. Figure 8.3 shows a cost

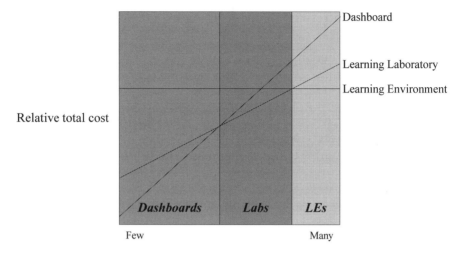

Number of people that will interface with the model

Figure 8.3 Learning Interface benefit-cost analysis.

evaluation for the three levels of interface and the most cost-efficient interface for the member of end users.

Dashboards are designed for the specific needs of each end user, thus the cost is mostly variable. This increases the cost with each end user added. LLs have a moderate fixed cost for developing the messaging within the simulator and a variable cost for developing the dashboard for each end user. LEs have a high fixed cost and relatively no variable costs as the intention is coached self-training, thus all users have the same dashboard interface.

We have found general support for the conclusion that as more people are involved with the model, the manner in which the learnings from the model are facilitated changes (see Figure 8.4). As the number of users increases, organizations move from teacher-facilitated sessions to more self-taught sessions. The teacher provides the 'learning environment,' so a dashboard interface might be sufficient. As the model develops, and the process becomes self-taught, then the learning environment needs to be added to the model, thus a learning environment interface might be more appropriate.

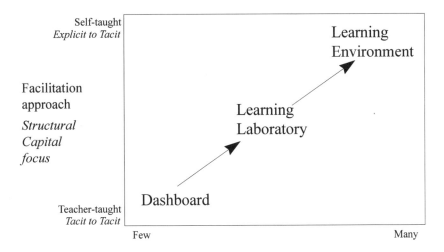

Number of people that will interface with the model

Figure 8.4 Appropriate Learning Interface for facilitation approach.

Case studies

The example Learning Laboratory presented in Figure 8.5 demonstrates how certain variables are user-defined in the simulator (the controls, such as average annual market growth and assembly labor) and others represent the results of the decisions made over time (the outputs, such as engine demand and engine gross profits).

LEVERAGE IN LEARNING INTERFACE DESIGN

Finding leverage in LIs focuses the designer's attention on getting more insight out of the LI for less investment of money and time. Current practice focuses on war gaming, which is examined below.

War gaming as a business opportunity

The term war gaming has become a popular term for simulations developed specifically for team problem solving and development. These simulations appear to offer substantial business opportunity. This information is not intended to expand upon your understanding

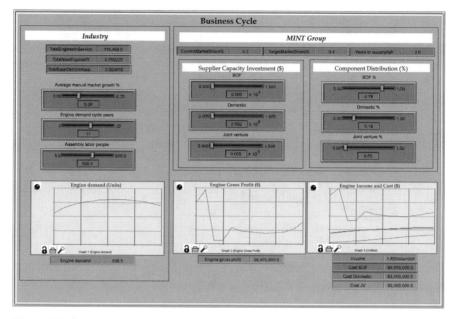

Figure 8.5 Sample Learning Laboratory Interface.

of systems thinking but rather to instill appreciation of the opportunities this field may offer.

War gaming is a term formerly associated with military planners that has moved to the corporate boardroom. War games, also referred to as executive flight simulators or learning environments, have increased in popularity in recent years with the combination of computer power and business modeling. This has yielded increasingly sophisticated, educational environments for executive and team learning.

Most corporations currently use computer simulation in training. Better software, more powerful computers, and programming languages, and more sophisticated computer users all support the inference that the use of computer simulation will continue to increase. Research indicates that all of the companies who use computer simulations purchase commercial simulations and most of those augment the commercial simulations with custom simulations.[2]

Recently, the Harvard Business School, in conjunction with High Performance Systems, began to market business-oriented system dynamics simulations. A generic business game written by Maxis, the company that wrote Sim-City, was introduced to favorable reviews. The generic business game market appears to be in the early stages of a boom.

The market for custom simulations is difficult to evaluate, since both the clients and developers tend to treat their activities as highly confidential. A growing trickle of magazine articles indicates a rapid growth in the use of computerized war games as a strategic development and learning tool for corporate management. The military, of course, develops and uses war games extensively. Large consulting firms, like Booz•Allen and Mercer, now have many years of experience in building war games for corporate clients. A number of small consulting firms also develop simulations and war games.

Information about custom war games is often anecdotal. Most games seem to involve ten to fifty participants and last one to two days. In some cases the game is used only once, in others the game is used repeatedly over time to investigate different problems and business environments. Many games are only marginally computerized and involve substantial human interpretation and involvement. This often slows the game such that only one scenario is explored in the one- or two-day session.

Typical custom war games may be used once or may be modified and used periodically. Technologies range from low-tech board games to sophisticated network-capable war games with specialized interfaces for each team (or team member). Many of the custom war games involve evaluation by consultants at each step to determine the input to a spreadsheet which 'gives validity' to the results and prints the output for the next round. Sophisticated tools are available for building computer based war games quickly and efficiently (software such as ithink, Vensim, and Powersim).

How does war gaming fit in?

System dynamics provides an efficient, speedy approach to war game design and implementation. System dynamics models can be built quickly and efficiently to capture the behavior of the system under study. The resulting model can be packaged in a simple, stand-alone 'game' for individuals or in more sophisticated, network-based games for teams. The system dynamics model can also be used to design an 'environment' for physical or 'board' games where computer use is not desired. System dynamics models are particularly useful in this latter situation for determining the values and the rules of the game to insure that interesting and educational behavior results in the play. Converting a system dynamics model to a war game or learning environment is relatively easy and offers potential extra value to both consulting teams and clients.

CHAPTER LEARNING SUMMARY

This chapter provided a framework for thinking about learning interfaces, and for understanding the many terms used in the field today. This section completes the Managing from Clarity process. We started by capturing our understanding of the system, analyzing the resulting causal map to identify hypothetical leverage points. We then simulated the map to test the hypotheses around each resource, as an integrated whole, and then under various scenarios. To communicate the insights developed throughout the process, we finished in this chapter with a Learning Interface with which others can share in the learning. The following chapters examine where this process can be applied and future directions of development.

Application Arenas　　　9

I am not sure where you can't apply Managing from Clarity.
(Two clients, both helping to lead cultural revolutions within large
organizations)

Now that we have completed the Managing from Clarity process, let us think about where the process can be applied. This chapter's purpose is to spark ideas on where Managing from Clarity would add the most value in the organization. We will look at five management efforts focused on adding value that are currently under way in many top organizations. They are performance measurement, negotiations, economic value added, corporate strategy, and high-velocity change. Top-selling books support each of these approaches. These approaches all focus on increasing organizational efficiency and effectiveness. Efficiency focuses on leveraging resource utilization, and effectiveness focuses on measuring the performance of complex social systems. For each approach, the section will describe how integrating these approaches with the Managing from Clarity process greatly enhances the value-added resulting from these types of initiatives.

PERFORMANCE MEASURES/BALANCED SCORECARD

Chapters 2 through 4 on GRASP Map and Analysis briefly explored the area of performance measurement. Based on the authors' work with the *Balanced Scorecard* leaders, Renaissance Worldwide, you will see how the Managing from Clarity approach strengthens the Balanced

Scorecard efforts. This brief introduction to systemic performance measurement should provide a clear picture of how current measurement systems, even when measuring different processes in an integrated fashion, do not determine which resources to focus on in a dynamic world of interrelated feedback systems.

Concept

In their best-selling book *The Balanced Scorecard: Translating Strategy into Action*, Robert Kaplan and David Norton demonstrate how the Balanced Scorecard provides decision-makers with a set of performance indicators that are linked causally to the organization's mission and strategy.[1] This strategic measurement and management system focuses on achieving financial objectives and the performance drivers of the financial objectives. This enables management to measure organizational performance across a balanced set of four perspectives. The four perspectives include financials, the customers that provide the income, the internal business processes with which the company services clients, and learning and growth, which provides human capital and technological support to continue to innovate the company's offering. This balanced set of measures permits decision-makers to track their financials while focusing on developing the resources and capabilities necessary for future growth.

To make the Balanced Scorecard work, Kaplan and Norton suggest that it is crucial to understand the cause–effect linkages between the performance drivers that decision-makers manage and the organization's strategic objectives. These linkages represent the organization's strategy, which Kaplan and Norton define as a set of hypotheses about cause and effect. They indicate that these relationships need to be made explicit so that they can be tested and managed. Kaplan and Norton suggest that in attempting to understand the cause–effect relationships between performance drivers and outcome measures, 'the Balanced Scorecard can be captured in a system dynamics model that provides a comprehensive, quantified model of a business's value creation process.'[2]

Leading enterprise system software companies, such as SAP and PeopleSoft have recently added an ability within the strategic enterprise management modules to use system dynamic modeling within a Balanced Scorecard sub-module. The interactive interfaces to the models in these software modules are learning environments, which were discussed in Chapter 8.[3]

Application of Managing from Clarity to the Balanced Scorecard

This section will now briefly demonstrate how the Managing from Clarity framework, language, and methodology adds value to the Balanced Scorecard. Specifically, we will look at balance, performance indicators, and cause–effect linkages, following the GRASP mental check. This section ends with an example of a Balanced Scorecard Learning Interface, which strengthens the strategy-making process.

Balanced objectives
The Global Goal and Stakeholder subgoals describe what the owners want the organization to achieve. By demonstrating how each stakeholder influences the organization's Global Goal, a balanced set of objectives is created among the stakeholders that directly affect the organization's survivability. Using balance to meet all Stakeholder Goals focuses organizational decision-making on the hard decisions of satisfying one stakeholder to the detriment of the others, or creating a balanced structure that meets the requirements of all stakeholders.

Selection of performance indicators
From the Enabling and Value-driving Resources, executives understand what resources they have, and which ones they need. From the Actions, executives understand what they are able to do and what they need to do to get the system going in the desired direction. The Managing from Clarity framework focuses decision-makers'

attention on the set of resources they need to monitor to drive value sustainably in a balanced manner.

Understanding and validating cause–effect linkages

From the Structure, executives explicitly understand how the enabling resources and performance drivers link causally to each other and to the organization's strategy. Finally, executives also develop a clear understanding of how People and their motivations affect the management of this system. This provides the explicit map of the organization with which people can understand and validate the linkages. The next step, as covered in Chapter 6, is to check the linkages and then test our dynamic hypotheses about them.

As seen in Chapter 8 on Learning Interfaces, a flight simulator may be developed to reflect the organization's Balanced Scorecard. Figure 9.1 shows an example Balanced Scorecard Learning Interface.

Case studies: dengue, Mint

In Chapter 4, the understanding of the organization from a systemic perspective provided insights into performance indicators for each

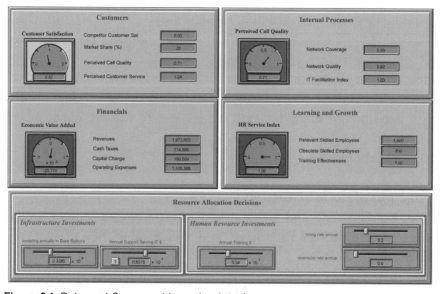

Figure 9.1 Balanced Scorecard Learning Interface.

area. The chapter discussed the current performance indicators for each group, and how they caused them to think about and manage the resources for which they were responsible and those they shared. We saw how the performance indicators determined the overall competency each group needed to achieve its goals. For example, Mint's marketing group was good at selling engines, and the Mexican municipal government traditionally focused on controlling costs and providing on-going services. In addition, the previous chapters showed how a systemic perspective of lagging and leading indicators provided a very different set of performance indicators for managing shared resources. Finally, we saw how summing up the core competencies of each group spoke to the type of organization we had designed. The Mint Company was traditionally strong at selling well-designed engines. The more systemic perspective suggested that, to leverage the organization's resources in achieving its global goal, the firm wanted to focus on designing and delivering engines the customers needed. This created a big change in focusing how management looked at using its enabling resources to drive value for its multiple stakeholders.

SYSTEMIC NEGOTIATIONS

Very complex negotiations that affect millions of lives for years to come occur daily within and among large organizations. These negotiations are handled generally by subject-matter-experts and negotiation-experts. The negotiations framework within which these experts work is largely intuition-based. Much work has been done in the last fifteen years to remedy this, but has done little to help these negotiators deal with highly complex decision environments. This section shows how the Managing from Clarity process provides a theoretical framework that improves a negotiator's understanding of the forces at work in the system being negotiated. This gives the negotiating team insight into the needs, demands, and abilities of the multiple actors involved.

World-class negotiation theory suggests that a 'win-win' or mutual gains perspective is more effective and efficient. 'Win-win' implies a dynamic understanding of the resources that two or more sides wish to accumulate over time. To understand the impact of different resources on one's success, and which resources one can and cannot give away, requires an integrated understanding of the business system and the value that those resources add in the system. Different personal experiences and backgrounds form the basis of this intuition of most negotiators and do not permit the level of integration that supports systemic negotiations.

Concept

The goal of negotiations, from the win-win, co-opetitive perspective, is to create 'value' for both parties. The prescribed best practice today is 'win-win' and BATNA,[4] which derive from Fisher and Ury's *Getting to Yes,* and from decision analysis in Raiffa's *The Art and Science of Negotiation* (1985).[5] These practices were derived from years of experience and research at the Harvard Negotiations Project, and represent a significant step forward for managers worldwide. In their simplicity, these models greatly enrich management's ability to negotiate stronger, more sustainable deals.

Negotiation is 'a process or course of treaty with another (or others) to obtain or bring about some result.'[6] In modern vernacular, negotiations are about gaining 'value' for all parties involved – two or more parties come together to negotiate only when they all stand to gain. Negotiation is used interchangeably with conflict resolution.

Professor Raiffa identifies negotiation characteristics, which greatly complicate one's negotiation preparation, including: number of parties, number of issues, repetitive games, and time constraints. As each of these characteristics increases in number, the resulting decision complexity increases. In complex, long-term projects such as an oil field development project or a business-to-business relationship, the parties involved negotiate: (1) the initial agreement (how much money will be given); (2) the policies governing during the negotiated time period (performance metrics and payment increases); and (3) the termination terms (under what conditions is the contract terminated, and how).

Most negotiation literature focuses on prescriptive approaches (the ten steps to success) and descriptive approaches (this is how I was successful). A few exceptions include Nash, Raiffa, Fisher, Ury and Patton. Nash (1950) introduced game theory into the bargaining literature, proposing axioms to achieve an acceptable solution for all parties. Raiffa (1985) applied decision analysis to assist in estimating one's own preferences and those of the opponent. Fisher, Ury and Patton (1991) present methodologies for better understanding the opponent's position and dealing systematically with complexity. These authors all focus on the initial negotiation, the first step. Lawyers often deal with terms of termination, the third step. However, none focus on understanding the policies governing the system between the initial and termination date, most likely because of the difficulty in dealing with the non-intuitive, non-linear behavior associated with complex systems.

Application of Managing from Clarity

Complex negotiations represent several difficulties for these best practices, such as multiple parties, high detail complexity, hidden needs of both parties, and changes over time. We briefly discuss how the negotiators could Negotiate from Clarity by applying the principles from the previous chapters.

Complex negotiations often have multiple parties each with their own interests. Existing methodologies often suffer under the weight of determining the best alternative for each party and where the many interests overlap. By making explicit the multiple stakeholders and what drives their satisfaction, the Managing from Clarity process already presents a framework for negotiating between multiple parties. Within the organization, management makes trade-offs to satisfy the requirements of multiple parties, who all have a stake in the outcomes of the organization. Likewise, within a negotiation, both sides make trade-offs to satisfy the requirements of other parties, who all have a stake in the outcome of the negotiation.

Complex negotiations often have high detail complexity, due to the many resources potentially included in the negotiation. Let's take an example. For a multinational oil company negotiating with a national government, resources under negotiation potentially include the obvious oil-related resources, such as mineral rights, equipment, property, human resources, technology, know-how, taxes, royalties, as well as non-obvious resources such as basic infrastructure, community development, and social impact studies. The difficulty of integrating these multiple factors into a negotiation has frustrated many negotiations where both groups might have benefited. As we have seen in previous chapters, the Managing from Clarity framework facilitates the integration of these multiple resources into an explicit map that indicates how these resources drive performance for the multiple stakeholders in the system.

In complex negotiations most parties often have needs that are never surfaced, yet these needs exert great pressures on them. For example, while the national government might be negotiating royalties with the oil company, the government might have a desperate need for high quality local education or infrastructure. If the negotiating team is aware of these needs, then they are in a stronger negotiating stance – maybe the oil company can provide the infrastructure or education more efficiently than the government and can offer that in exchange for royalties. The point is that needs that go undiscovered cannot be satisfied in a win-win negotiation. By mapping out a GRASP Map for each of the parties involved, the negotiating team more strongly understands the issues each party faces.

The last major issue we will address regarding complex negotiations focuses on how resource requirements and availability change over time. Most of the formal negotiation literature focuses on understanding the multiple attributes of a decision-maker's BATNA, but only at time 0, not over time.[7] As we have seen throughout this book, organizations create value for their stakeholders through multiple, interrelated resources. These resources rise and fall over time, and these changes affect flows that depend on those resources. These dependent flows in kind affect their related resources. As this is all changing over time, strategic issues vary over time. As an example, the organization will focus on the inflow of new customers in the beginning, as they represent the vast majority of the customer base. Over time, though, strategic emphasis will begin to shift from growing to maintaining the customer base. The shift in resource priorities over time should be considered in the negotiation. For example, the government might request that in the beginning the oil company train local nationals to operate the pipeline, and then after a few years, the government will need training in how to maintain and upgrade the pipeline. These skills are useless in the beginning and crucial later on in the project. Both sides could gain by including these types of long-term resource issues.

Addressing the multiple issues just raised, we can apply the Managing from Clarity process to the strategic process of developing a negotiating posture. Table 9.1 shows the Negotiating from Clarity procedure.

Benefit-cost analysis of Negotiating from Clarity

When developing a negotiating strategy, negotiators face the same constraints all decision-makers face, how to develop a strong plan at the lowest cost. From a benefit-cost perspective, there are basically three levels of systemic understanding a team can use to support the negotiation. First, as we saw in Chapter 3, simply capturing how the negotiating team thinks about the system in a qualitative systemic resource map (QualMap) provides insight into the relevant issues and provides a map for thinking through how the issues interrelate. This is a very low-cost strategy. Second, completing the GRASP Map and Analysis step focuses the team on the perspectives of the different stakeholders involved in the system, how they will impact possible negotiation stances, and which negotiation points provide the strongest leverage for all parties involved – these are very impactful insights. This second level requires a bit more time of the team. The third level develops the team's insight all the way through

Table 9.1 Negotiating from Clarity process.

Step	Action undertaken
Analysis	Understand needs and reservation values for all parties involved
1	GRASP negotiation context from the perspective of all negotiating parties
2	Identify benefit leverage points, BATNA, reservation values for all parties
3	Model each party's preferences
4	Run sensitivity analysis on leverage points
5	Formulate preliminary negotiation strategies
6	Scenario planning
7	Formulate final negotiation strategy
Planning	Formulate negotiation strategy
1	Decide what information to share with the other parties to the negotiation. Decide whether or not to integrate their thinking and how
2	Iterate the model, integrating the new learnings and requirements at each step, knowing what you can give away, what you cannot, and what they can and cannot
Action	Negotiate
1	Win-win the negotiation
2	Iterate on models during negotiations

the Managing from Clarity process, through the GRASP Map and Analysis, key resource dynamics, resource integration steps, scenario planning, and Learning Interface development. This provides the team with additional insight into the dynamics over time of resource development and an understanding of *how much* and *when*, as well as a robust understanding of the issues to be tackled and the strongest leverage points over time. This third level requires a significant investment of the team's time, and is most appropriate for negotiations affecting significant investments of resources or long-term projects, where uncertainty is highest.

ECONOMIC VALUE ADDED

For many years, senior management has focused on their ability to meet stockholder expectations. As organizations increased in complexity and increased the market capitalization, executives required ever more sophisticated financial measures. One of the latest is the concept of economic value added (EVA).[8]

EVA is significantly strengthened by linking it to a dynamic model of the organization. This section briefly presents the concept of EVA and then presents some examples of how the Managing from Clarity process strengthens the identification of value creation drivers, and where and how managers should intervene in the system, to add the most value to the organization's global goal of value maximization.

Concept

The concept of economic value added is quite straightforward, to create value for its stockholders, a firm's profits must exceed the cost of capital. The cost of capital can be seen as an opportunity cost – will the investment make more than it costs? Application of EVA is quite a bit more complicated. As yet there are no universally accepted standards about what to include as economic capital nor how. Economic capital represents the resources that the firm has invested in and is depreciating over time. A prime difficulty is determining which resources to include and how to measure them. To calculate the value of discounted EVA over time, firms now use the Market Value Added (MVA). The typical method calculates potential cash flow streams, as if for a traditional NPV[9] calculation, and based on a cost of capital, discounts the future EVA's for a cumulative MVA. These calculations are usually based on complicated models of the business and projected cash flows.

Application of Managing from Clarity

Combined with the EVA framework, Managing from Clarity becomes a potent tool with which policymakers have a dynamic financial understanding of the policies that create value for the organization, in the form of positive EVA. Not only can executives measure whether certain policies will create value over time, executives can also determine which policies will create the most value over time. How is this different from the cash flow projection models used for typical MVA calculations? QuantMaps make it much easier to model, to calculate, and thus to decide what to include in the EVA calculation. Let us explore each briefly. First, it is straightforward to calculate EVA from the flow and accumulation of resources in the QuantMap, thus the EVA is automatically calculated WHILE the policymakers runs through all of the analyses that we have seen throughout this book. In other words, EVA becomes another calculation used to determine the value created by different policies. Second, as is clear by now, the investments (actions) organizations make in their enabling resources affect many other Enabling and Value-Driving Resources throughout the organization. This interrelatedness requires that future cash-flow projections calculate these interrelated effects over time, which is complicated to do in most simulation models and quite difficult in spreadsheet models. However, we have seen that it is quite easy to model systems of interdependent resources using the system dynamics approach. Thus, since it is easier to model and work with, the QuantMap also facilitates the process of deciding what factors to include in the EVA calculation.

CORPORATE STRATEGY

In their (1998) textbook *Corporate Strategy: A Resource-Based Approach*, Professors Collis and Montgomery revealed that their research showed that the corporate management in more than half of the forty organizations interviewed could not effectively describe how their activities added value to the firms in their corporation![10] To address this issue, Collis and Montgomery demonstrate how a resource-based view of the corporation provides a framework that clarifies corporate management's role in value creation.

Concept

Collis and Montgomery distinguish between corporate and business-level strategy. Corporate strategy focuses on the overall strategy for a diversified company, while business-level strategy focuses on building a competitive advantage in a discrete and identifiable market. Corporate strategists create value by structuring and coordinating the corporation's multimarket activities. This highlights three key concepts: value creation, structuring, and coordination. Value creation focuses on bringing resources together to create value, in the businesses. Structuring focuses on strategic clarity: the direction of sustainable value creation in a competitive environment. Coordination focuses on administrative clarity: how the business is running, against projections, and strategic implementation.

However, Collis and Montgomery propose that valuable resources can only be identified through a data-intensive, process-oriented analysis of the organization's resources. This time-intensive search through stacks of data will not ferret out the key relationships between strategic resources, identify the resources with highest leverage over time, nor contemplate the effects of local rationales on resource accumulation. By providing these specific attributes in a more intuitive, user-friendly process, the Managing from Clarity process adds systemic rigor to the powerful corporate design concepts developed by Collis and Montgomery.

Application of Managing from Clarity[11]

Applying the Managing from Clarity framework highlights three areas that strengthen corporate strategy: (1) a resource map that clearly delineates how the different corporate staff functions create value for the corporation; (2) discovery of the high-leverage components of the corporate strategy; and (3) corporate roles and performance measurement.

Resource map

As in the previous chapters, a GRASP Map starts with the Global Goal, which for a corporation might be to maximize the sustainable potential for value creation. Sustainable value creation might be calculated as the corporation's Market Value Added (MVA), which is a function of the firm's EVA and probability for survival. As seen in the EVA section above, Value-Driving Resources in the firms determine the EVA of each firm, while the sustainability of the competitive advantage and corporate risk profile determine corporate survivability. The Value-Driving Resources for the corporate risk profile, at first blush, focus on the corporation's ethics, access to capital, changes in the social–political–competitive environment, and the corporation's flexibility facing the environment. The corporate-level staff enact structuring activities that take Action on the Enabling Resources of the firms, and coordinating activities that affect the systems which evaluate the firm's performance and determine overall corporate strategy. The results of these Actions on the Enabling Resources, and subsequently on the Value-Driving Resources, affect the Stakeholder Goals and then the Global Goal. As the potential for value creation increases, the corporation's owners choose whether to reinvest in the Actions. This GRASP Map clearly positions the three corporate roles and how they add value to the businesses, where value is created, as stated above.

High-leverage components of corporate strategy

As just shown, it is straightforward to model the relationship between the corporate resources and the business units they serve. The previous chapters demonstrated, with various examples, how to identify subjective and objective leverage points within the system, moving step by step through the Managing from Clarity process.

Corporate roles and performance measurement

Developing a GRASP Map of the corporate function, three different, interrelated roles gain clarity: observers, implementers, and designers. Observers are the custodians of the Global Goal and the Stakeholder subgoals. The observers integrate and report corporate results to the organization's owners or stockholders. Implementers are responsible for the value-creating resources and the enabling resources. Implementers collaborate with the businesses to create value, as part of the implementation team. Designers are responsible for the actions, the structure, and the people. Designers focus on the design of the

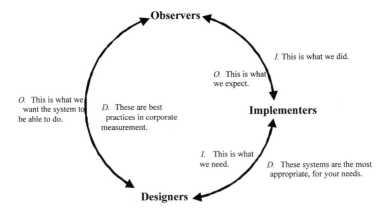

Figure 9.2 How the three corporate roles interrelate.

structures and systems that the coordinators use to create value. These three groups have various supplier/customer expectations with each other that create their interrelationships, as captured in Figure 9.2. This diagram makes clear that different corporate staff members make significantly different contributions to the organization, and have different expectations about the roles of the others in the corporate group.

Performance criteria often map against delivery expectations to an individual's clients and suppliers inside and outside of the organization. Since it is obvious that people should be evaluated for what they do, and how activity contributes value to the organization, each of these three roles should have different evaluation criteria. For example, based on the client/supplier relationships the designer has with the observers and the implementers, the designer should be evaluated on the success of their design of corporate measurement systems and coordination systems, not on the implementation or reporting itself, as they are not responsible for that area.

HIGH-VELOCITY CHANGE

In their (1998) book *Competing on the Edge: Strategy as Structured Chaos*, Brown and Eisenhardt describe a revolutionary view of how to strategize in organizations facing intense, high-velocity change.[12] They argue that success derives from the ability for firms to manage transitions and rhythm in highly dynamic industries.

Concept

Traditional strategy focuses on the development of sustainable competitive advantage. In high-velocity environments, these advantages are quickly copied or made obsolete by the competition, often within months. Traditionally the strategy process extends over months as the organization identifies, often in excruciating detail, its external threats, and opportunities in the marketplace, and its internal strengths and weaknesses. Then it develops a plan of attack and puts together a budget to meet the plan. The information systems required to monitor achievement of the plan follow. In the time that it takes to develop this process, one time around, organizations in high-velocity environments have already changed strategic focus two to three times. So the traditional process is not helpful for them. Brown and Eisenhardt pull from complexity and evolutionary theory, as well as the nature of speed and time-pacing to explain how successful companies in high-velocity environments thrive.

These theories provide a basis from which to think about how to create structural flexibility to the environment through a balance between very structured, stable organizations and completely unstructured organizations. This focuses management on what to structure and what not to structure. Another key concept, time, focuses on how to create an organization that can change focus quickly while having built up enough resources to provide high quality products and services efficiently. The third key concept, pace of change, focuses management on the rate of change required to constantly be ahead of the game – the organization is not changing now to find some comfortable place to stabilize, the organization will always be changing at a certain pace.

Application of Managing from Clarity

The Managing from Clarity process provides three key tools for managers in high-velocity environments: (1) time-efficient strategy; (2) a platform for shared strategy; and (3) maps with which to communicate strategy.

Time-efficient strategy

As Brown and Eisenhardt highlight, time is a key constraint for organizations facing high-velocity environments. The Managing from Clarity process has been developed and tested with organizations in many industries, with the intent of developing intuitive, quick-to-use tools that provide policy-makers with clarity about their organizations. These tools provide fast organizations with a map of their intent with which they can communicate the plan of attack. As important as what was just said, is what was not said. The map is not fixed for all time. The map can change as the demands on the organization change, since the map can be developed and modified relatively quickly. This reveals another key feature of GRASP Maps in high-velocity environments – the map's degree of stability. Strategists often complain that everything is changing; but the essence of the question is, what is really changing and at what speed?

From the GRASP perspective, what is changing in the organization? The Global Goal and Stakeholder Goals tend to be constant, even in high-velocity environments. Stockholders still want impossibly high returns. Customers want more, better and different. Employees want excitement and fair pay. So the goals are pretty stable over time. All organizations use the same basic Enabling Resources such as people, skills, money, physical assets, and technology, so these are pretty stable. What changes significantly in high-velocity environments? – How the organization creates value for its stakeholders and the actions required to create that value. An organization might provide one product today and a completely different product or service six months later. The Goals are the same and many of the Enabling Resources remain the same, only the Value-Driving Resources have changed. This means that the organization's GRASP Map of its business does not have to be completely redone every couple of months, rather only how its Enabling Resources create value to achieve the Stakeholder subgoals as their high velocity change takes the organization to the next level of play.

Platform for shared strategy

Venture capitalists (VC) say that one of the key attributes they look for in a start-up has nothing to do with the initial business plan, which they know will change within the first six months anyway. The VCs want to see how the management team works together. Do they communicate well? Will they be able to stick together and figure out how to surmount the inevitable, often-seemingly-impossible obstacles to come? A key issue in strategy development in high-velocity environments deals with getting everyone on the same page. The GRASP Map captures the perspective of all the different groups in the organization and how together they orchestrate the Enabling Resources that integrate to create value for the organization's multiple stakeholders. VCs find the ability to get on the same page as crucial to the success of high-velocity ventures.

Maps to communicate strategy

A third crucial component of managing organizations in high-velocity environments centers on the ability to communicate clearly to the organizations stakeholders what the organization is focusing on and why. Employees and investors both want to understand how their valuable resources are being used. The Managing from Clarity process adds that clarity and provides the tools with which to communicate it to internal stakeholders, such as other managers and employees, as well as external stakeholders such as investors.

CHAPTER LEARNING SUMMARY

Many theories of management are evolving to help policy-makers think more strategically about their organizations in ever-more competitive environments. As has been shown, the Managing from Clarity process does not replace these theories, rather, it provides a process and systemic perspective for implementing them. This chapter has shown that the powerful Managing from Clarity framework strengthens thinking about how to organize complex systems combined with the top management theories, resulting in a strong tool to increase organizational efficiency and effectiveness sustainably.

Future Developments: **10**
The Strategist

> Managing from Clarity is what we do every day anyway, we just don't
> know it.
>
> (A senior staff engineer at Royal Dutch/Shell)

In the previous chapters, we explored the Managing from Clarity process and management tools it strengthens. In this chapter, we change focus from the tools and applications to the person applying the tools of strategic management – the strategist or organizational designer.

Why do some employees perform poorly? Most managers would answer that question by ticking off a list that includes weak skills, insufficient experience, inability to prioritize assignments, and lack of motivation. In other words, they would contend that poor performance is the employee's fault. But is it?

Not always, according to Manzoni and Barsoux, the authors of the *Harvard Business Review* article 'The Set-up-to-Fail Syndrome.'[1] Their research with hundreds of executives strongly suggests that it is the bosses themselves – albeit unintentionally – who are frequently responsible for an employee's subpar achievement.

According to Manzoni and Barsoux, bosses and their perceived weak performers are often caught in a dynamic called the set-up-to-fail syndrome, which tends to play out as follows: A boss begins to worry when a subordinate's performance is not satisfactory. He then takes what seems like the obvious action by increasing the time and attention he focuses on the employee. Rather than improve the subordinate's performance, the increased supervision has the reverse effect. The subordinate, in perceiving the boss's lack of confidence in him, withdraws from his work and from the boss. Moreover, the relationship spirals downward. We would suggest that any reader of this book has probably experienced one side or the other of this at some point in their career.

What is a boss to do? First, he or she must accept the possibility that their own behavior could be contributing to the problem. Second, he or she must plan a careful intervention with the subordinate that takes the form of one or several candid conversations meant to untangle the unhealthy dynamics in the relationship. The intervention is never easy, but the time and energy invested in it usually yields a high payback.

THE NEED FOR A CERTIFIED CORPORATE DESIGNER (CCD)

The Manzoni and Barsoux article discusses personal dynamics as one critical reason for employee underperformance. We propose that there are not only personality issues at hand but also organizational design issues at hand. As we discussed in Chapter 2 in the Theory of the Firm, it is management's responsibility to structure the linkages among the different areas of the organization to achieve the firm's Global Goal. Given that design is their job, we forward the development of the Certified Corporate Designer concept as a qualification mechanism for entry into senior management.

Why the need?

As seen often in Forbes, CEOs are hired for their expected leadership skills and fired based on their inability to affect the same miracle again in a different setting. The focus of this dialog is often about leadership skills and vision (or lack of) and rarely discusses the nitty gritty of organizational design that facilitates getting the job done. Charisma alone is not enough. The true question to answer is, why can the same leader consistently redesign companies in different industries and others cannot? It cannot be that they understand the details of every industry and we mere mortals are blind. Though innate, these leaders have a keen sense of understanding structures that will succeed and those that will fail in a given environment.

This skill is the same knowledge and skill that architects and physicians must have. We depend upon these architects to provide consistently stable structures and doctors to provide consistent treatments for the same pathologies. We demand this consistency from them so that our buildings do not fall down and our health is stable. Why are they licensed and senior managers not?

Given the responsibility leadership teams have to provide consistent returns in turbulent times, we suggest that these corporate design capabilities be considered as a distinct skill that contributes to their success. We suggest that this skill is not only interesting, but also essential and needs to be incorporated formally into corporate management's skill set. In this way, those who want to pursue a career in corporate management will have a clear understanding of one skill set that will contribute to their ability to consistently structure their organization for consistent performance over time.

What are the qualifications?

The qualifications we propose for the Corporate Designer certification are based on hard as well as soft organizational design principles. These include: people, systems thinking, performance measurement, economics, and organizational structures. Let us briefly describe each one.

People

Since it is the people that do the work, not the organization, it is imperative to explicitly understand the individual goals and needs of the individuals who are working in each major building block of the organization. The Managing from Clarity framework expands the traditional human resources understanding of 'people' from line workers and staff workers to include the multiple key actors that influence and drive the organization. These tend to include external actors, such as investors, shareholders, government agencies and clients as well as internal actors as indicated by their contribution to getting things done (functional areas such as production, distribution, and sales). Identifying these external and internal actors ensures that policy-makers include the most important forces that interact with and within the organization. Training in organizational psychology and group dynamics support this area of understanding for the certification of the Corporate Designer.

Systems thinking

The discipline of systems thinking provides the rigorous methodology and toolset for capturing the critical linkages among these key actors in a transparent and useful way. By focusing on the elements of feedback and delays inherent in the movement of material across these linkages, systems thinking offers a new approach to understanding the impacts of sensible actions in one part of the organization on unwitting members of another part of the organization. The unexpected consequences often disrupt and derail important initiatives and provoke internal conflicts within the organization around shared resources. The ability to explore the roots of these conflicts in systemic terms also provides corporate management with the insight into modifying the organization's structure in order to alleviate or minimize these conflicts. In addition, the tools of systems thinking provide a consistent basis for testing design ideas in a safe environment before putting the organization through the painful and often traumatic experience of sequential corporate restructuring. Much has been written (and lived) around this issue.

Performance measurement

From the management axiom 'you cannot manage what you cannot measure,' tremendous efforts have been spent on understanding and implementing new performance management systems. Great confusion has been created in the organization between this concept as a means or as an end, when implementing such management tools as SAP, the Balanced Scorecard, and Economic Value Added (EVA).

For the corporate designer, performance measurement is a means for the leadership team to do the following:

- Communicate what is important for the firm, from the corporate management perspective.
- Track progress of on-going initiatives.
- Gain insight into potentially new areas for development.

Training in IT as a decision-support tool (versus merely a reporting tool) and studies in organizational behavior to understand how to place appropriate incentives throughout the firm would support the Corporate Designer certification.

Economics

Training in economics will provide the Corporate Designer with a deeper understanding of the traditional forces that drive performance among competitors and industries. The theoretical backdrop offers a consistent, studied response to why the world works as it does. It also provides designers with specific tools to help them construct the logic behind the critical linkages the firm has with the market and with its shareholders. Making this understanding explicit gives the designer another tool to communicate their ideas with the rest of the firm.

Organizational structures

The study of organizational structures provides the Designer with a consistent set of principles with which to build the foundation for the organization depending upon the specific needs of that industry and market position. A start-up firm requires very different design from a mature business. Each has their complexity, and the role of the Corporate Designer is to understand the transitions that need to be made, and when, in the development of the firm. Here is where the design principles have an added complexity – the requirements for design must include flexibility and awareness of the firm's place in time regarding its own growth.

QUALIFICATIONS FOR THE CERTIFIED CORPORATE DESIGNER

The Managing from Clarity approach provides a very strong foundation for the appointment of the Certified Corporate Designer. As seen in Chapters 3, 4 and 5, the GRASP methodology supports each one of these five requirements. By focusing on the *Goals*, the policy-maker looks at the integration between the global goal of the organization and the individual goals of the people who do the work. By considering *Resources*, the Managing from Clarity approach incorporates the main economic and operational drivers that accelerate, maintain, and inhibit the firm's performance over time. By focusing on the *Actions* people take within these structures, this approach takes a systems thinking view of the firm by addressing the issues of feedback and delay of actions taken across the firm over time. By considering *Structures*, the approach studies the organization's structure and how stresses and stimulants in one part of the structure affect other parts of the firm, both in expected and unexpected ways. By looking at *People*, the process provides the Corporate Designer with tools to consider which incentives and where to place them across the organization in order to achieve the overarching goal of the firm.

In summary, the role of a Certified Corporate Designer is appropriate for an introduction into senior management. This will create a more consistent basis for senior management to consider the design issues they face when stepping into a leadership position. The Managing from Clarity approach offers a fundamentally important role in the development of the Certified Corporate Designer in that it addresses the five main thrusts of knowledge the Designer should have: people, systems thinking, performance measurement, economics, and organizational structures.

Notes

Chapter1

1   In the private sector, the authors have worked with companies in the petroleum, electronic commerce, electric utility, health care, insurance, mining, telecommunications, aerospace, management consulting, retail, food, and banking industries. In the public sector, we have worked with national and state health services, municipality governments, and urban planning initiatives. The organizations have varied from Global Fortune 500 firms and national governmental agencies in Europe, North America, Central America, South America, Asia and Africa to a mom and pop store and town management.

2   Various schools of 'theories of the firm' exist (i.e., behavioral, economic, legal, resource-based, knowledge-based) (Holmstrom and Tirole, 1989, 65).

3   Seminal research on the resource-based view concepts presented here can be found in: Andrews (1971); Arrow (1974); Dierickx and Cool (1989); and Wernerfelt (1984).

4   See Dierickx and Cool (1989); Glucksman, Mollona, and Morecroft (1997).

5   Examples from Wernerfelt (1984).

6   Quote from PM Network, September 1997, cited in the February 23, 1998 issue of *LEVERAGE*, published by Pegasus Communications.

7   Dynamic complexity increases as the distance between cause and effect increases in time and space.

8   For many examples, see Peter Senge's best seller (1990).

9   See Barnard (1968, 19).

10   The concept of cause–effect is familiar to all managers, but usually presented in a statistical or probabilistic format. The focus is on the cause–effect relationship only between X and Y. Systems thinking focuses on the feedback and delays inherent in multiple cause–effect relationships.

11   See Gouillart and Kelly (1995); Kaplan and Norton (1996).

12   Jay W. Forrester at MIT founded system dynamics in the 1950s to apply his knowledge of feedback systems in engineering to social systems. His seminal work in the field is Industrial Dynamics (Forrester, 1961).

13   See Meadows (1980, 31–32), where Donella Meadows defines feedback as follows.

> It is assumed that social or individual decisions are derived from information about the state of the system or environment surrounding the decision maker. The

decisions lead to actions that are intended to change the state of the system. New information about the changed state (or unchanged, if the action has been ineffective) then produces further decisions and changes. Each such closed chain of causal relationships forms a feedback loop.

For those interested in the history of feedback thought, see Richardson (1991).

14   See Vennix (1996). Delays play a crucial role in systems. The desired insight about delays is that shorter (or immediate) response is not necessarily better. See Morecroft (1983) for applications of this concept to supply chain management and MRP systems. Nobel Laureate Herbert Simon (1997) shows that the stimulus-response mode promotes non-rationality versus a hesitation-choice mode, which permits rationality to be brought into the focus of attention.

15   See Conner (1991).

16   The case studies present actual projects completed by the authors.

17   The Mint case study presented in this book represents a 'sanitized' version of real problems faced by real companies in the capital equipment manufacturing industries.

Chapter 2

1   MIT Professor John Sterman argues this point very strongly (Sterman, 1991). See also Smith (1989).

2   The importance of problem structuring in all fields has been exhaustively documented. See also Forrester (1961), Keeney (1992), and Simon (1997).

3   Many elicitation methods exist. An experienced facilitator will have a suite of methods for extracting this information, using the one most appropriate for the situation.

4   This is the technical term used in system dynamics, also called a reference mode or a reference mode of behavior. Refer to Forrester (1961), and Richardson and Pugh (1981).

5   This dynamic is described in more detail in Ritchie-Dunham (1999).

6   Harvard's Professor Chris Argyris (1993) differentiates between Theories-in-Use and Espoused Theories.

7   This method pulls heavily from the means–ends objectives network, from Keeney (1992).

8   According to Kelly (1963, 8–9):

> Man looks at his world through transparent patterns or templates which he creates and then attempts to fit over the realities of which the world is composed. The fit is not always very good. Yet without such patterns the world appears to be such an undifferentiated homogeneity that man is unable to make any sense out of it. Even a poor fit is more helpful to him than nothing at all.

9   For causal-loop diagram 'how to' manuals and theory, a basic component of system dynamics, refer to Richardson and Pugh (1981), and Roberts *et al.* (1983).

10   To learn how to develop detailed causal maps, see the multiple references available at Pegasus Communications http://www.pegasuscom.com/, the leading publisher of systems thinking newsletters and manuals.

11   Alternatively, the arrow may be read as 'affects' or 'influences.' For our purposes the descriptions of causes, effects, or influences can be used relatively interchangeably. Aside from the obvious connotative differences, the words are essentially the same, and add richness to the cause–effect explanation.

12   Chapter 5 on Key Resource Dynamics will show that this seemingly circular causality is really quite obvious and relevant. For now it will suffice to say that the circular causality is not really circular as there are some implied intermediate variables missing. Specifically, *supplier productivity* affects *supplier output* now, where as significant increases in *supplier output* for the same level of *supplier labor* taxes the *supplier labor* over time, bringing about a decrease in the average *supplier productivity*.

13   The actual exercise included other relationships, excluded here to simplify the explanation.

14   This reinforcing behavior also works in the upward direction. If the spin becomes positive, then it reinforces the 'good' behavior.

15   Actually the reinforcing force of the gravitational pull and the compensating force of the friction, neglecting other forces, net to an increasing positive force, as the snowball grows, rolling down the hill.

16   Nonaka and Takeuchi (1995) emphasize the importance of being able to capture the implicit information in the heads of different experts and making it tacit, so that it can be communicated to the rest of the group.

17   For two particularly powerful discussions of this matter provided by consulting researchers, see Andersen and Richardson (1997), and Vennix (1996).

Chapter 3

1   This framework agrees with the work done by University of Minnesota Professor Andrew H. Van de Ven (1987, 339–340) in which he proposes that any good theory of the strategic management of change requires an explanation of: (1) how structure and individual purposive action are linked at micro and macro-levels of analysis; (2) how change is produced both by the internal functioning of the structure and by the external purposive actions of individuals; (3) the structure under conditions of both stability and instability; and (4) time as the key historical metric, including both *chronos* (calendar time) and *kiros* (periods of peak performance).

2   Archetype is defined in Webster's as 'An original model or type after which other similar things are patterned; a prototype. An ideal example of a type.'

3   See Daniel Kim, System Archetypes I, Pegasus Communications, or Appendix 2 of Peter Senge's *The Fifth Discipline* (1990), for a full description of the most common archetypes, their typical behavior and how to best attack them.

4   This empirical finding is somewhat substantiated by the widespread use and success that many systems thinking groups have had with the use of archetypes. See The Systems Thinker by Pegasus Communications, and Senge (1990).

5   An interesting approach to teaching people about the behavior of feedback structures is shown in an example provided by Michael Radzicki (1992).

6   A summary of these findings is presented in the global and local perspective sections of this chapter.

7   Reading QualMap invokes *ceteris paribus*, a term used in economics to mean 'all else remaining the same.' An increase in Supplier Output will correspond with an increase in Assembly, as long as Production Capacity is sufficient and constant. This is the accepted way to read QualMaps.

8   New theoretical frameworks for understanding which feedback loops or 'paths' are dominating the behavior of any given variable will be shown in Chapter 6 on Resource Integration.

9   See Goodman (1974), for a mathematical explanation of 'overshoot and collapse.'

10   These three analytical tools are applied to the QualMap, which was developed over two weeks with the team.

11   This exercise continues to provide some of the most shocking insight to management teams. The archetypes have confirmed global dynamics they were half-expecting. At this stage, they are then confronted with the fact that the structure of policies that they have put in place (the causal map in which they now believe) shows that the locally rational goals often provide counterproductive forces to achieving global goals. See Ritchie-Dunham and Membrillo (1999) for more examples.

12   Physical capacity increases are decided annually or biannually in this industry, providing a very significant delay between need to respond and ability to respond. Adjusting the assembly labor force requires six months of training to bring a new worker up to expert levels of productivity.

13   This idea was developed by Peter Scott-Morgan (1994).

14   From the authors' experience, the global and local perspectives often provide shockingly different views of the same system.

15   In James Quinn's studies of organizations, he found that management primarily dealt with growth and uncertainty through small incremental changes (Quinn, 1980).

16   Many authors write about change as the new constant. This new focus on change is due to the extreme growth that occurred in the 1990s. At high levels of growth, management spends relatively more and more time making incremental changes and less and less on managing the resource efficiency, which is their principal responsibility.

Chapter 4

1   We refer to the 'system manager' as the person managing the system being modeled. We clarify this to avoid other uses of the word, derived from the widespread use of 'system' in the information technology world.

2   Several authors (Dupperin and Godet, 1975; Duval and Gabus, 1975; Georgantzas and Acar, 1995; Ritchie-Dunham, 1997) have investigated the application of Godet's MICMAC (Matrice d'Impacts Croisés Multiplication Appliquée à un Classement, which translates as Cross-Impact Matrix Multiplication Applied to Classification) analysis to systems analysis. The authors have developed software that automates the development and analysis of the MICMAC matrix.

3   To normalize means to take the highest value from all of the variables and make it equal to 1. All other values are then represented as a percent of the highest value.

4   This terminology was proposed by Georgantzas *et al.* (Georgantzas and Acar, 1995).

5   From the authors' experience, the MICMAC analysis typically about 15% of the variables fall in Quadrant #1, 5% in Quadrant #2, 30% in Quadrant #3, and 50% in Quadrant #4.

6   First, all variables in the model are important, otherwise they would not have been included. Therefore, a variable's relative influence and exposure are by no means related to importance, rather, its leverage over time.

7   We thank Scott Spann for the creative names placed in parentheses to identify the key strategy for the variables in each quadrant.

8   This relic of a past paradigm is further evidence for the resource-based perspective that resources also form a firm's memory, in this case, cost cutting. Resources are built up over time, and they have to be drained over time – they cannot be filled or emptied instantaneously. For example, to have a high level of employee satisfaction requires that this resource be built up over time and maintained or it will drain, over time.

9   Erling Moxnes won the prestigious Jay W. Forrester Award for showing, among other things, how misperceptions in strategic management often result from different perspectives on which 'enabling' resources affect different inputs or outputs to the 'value-driving' resources (Moxnes, 1998). See Ritchie-Dunham and Membrillo (2000) for another example of the Stakeholder Relationship Assessment.

10   Refer to *Leverage* (Pegasus Communications) 2/9/98 'Resource Library' for the effect of performance indicators on system behavior.

11   Behavioral research has found the use of group goals to improve performance, when employees are interdependent. See Mitchell and Silver (1990); O'Leary-Kelly, Martocchio, and Frink (1994).

12   Robert Kaplan and David Norton, authors of the bestseller *The Balanced Scorecard* (1996) emphasize the importance of a systemic approach to performance measurement, as evidenced by their recent addition of a systems thinking Learning Environment based on their book, and a whole section in their most recent book (2000).

13   In the Introduction, we stated that a key requirement of direct leverage was low dynamic complexity (low cause-effect distance in time and space). This condition is most often met at the local perspective level.

Chapter 5

1   The Key Resource Dynamics methodology relies heavily on the system dynamics stock-flow modeling language (Forrester, 1961; Sterman, 2000). This approach to mapping out the dynamics around resources allows modelers to use expert intuition and implicit understanding of the system to map out the resource dynamics in a highly systematic, concise, interrelated and comprehensive fashion. We contrast this approach with those of game theory that require Herculean intellects and two-by-two matrices to document exhaustively the interrelated mechanisms for affecting a resource.

2   Jay W. Forrester (1961) argues that it is impossible to begin to understand the effects of policies without simulating. The authors agree, suggesting that qualitative approaches allow

us to capture and understand the overall behavior of complex systems, in an efficient fashion; then we simulate to test our understanding.

3   Herbert Simon (1997) showed that humans are bounded rationally. This directly applies to the ability of humans to simulate, in their heads, the interactions, and dynamics of multiple parts moving at the same time.

4   See Warren (1997).

5   See the chapter on Mental Models in Senge (1990).

6   We strongly recommend the following books for an introduction to the principles of stock-flow modeling (Forrester, 1961; Forrester, 1990; Goodman, 1974; Sterman, 2000).

7   See the Creative Learning Exchange at http://www.mit.edu/sds/cle.html for more information on the System Dynamics K-12 program.

8   This reflects the fundamental law of physics, that we cannot create matter.

9   In ordinary differential equations, we would describe this system with the following two equations:

$$\dot{m} = t_l^{-1} l - [t_{m,d}^{-1} + (e_{m,c} + e_{m,i})(1 - t_{m,d}^{-1})]m$$

$$\dot{l} = 0.5 t_{m,o}^{-1} m - [t_l^{-1} + e_{l,i}(1 - t_l^{-1})]l$$

$$\text{where} \quad \dot{m} = \frac{dm}{dt}.$$

10   The mathematical equivalent of a stock is X and a flow is dX/dt.

11   Note that qualitative systemic resource maps (QualMaps) do not differentiate between stocks and flows, focusing solely on the stocks, with the flows implicit in the arrows. When we convert QualMaps to key resource dynamics diagrams, we necessarily add more variables.

12   When stopped instantaneously, a stock might have a value of zero, because at that moment there is nothing in it, (e.g. there are no mosquitoes right now), but at another stopped instant, there might be something in it, therefore it is still a stock.

13   The authors thank Barry Richmond for this term. He differentiates between operational thinking (how things work) and correlational thinking (laundry listing).

14   Many managers would not consider orders in process a resource. However, Dierickx and Cool (1989) define a resource as an 'asset stock,' in the most global sense, as anything that accumulates. This differentiates a 'resource' from a 'strategic resource,' which is a resource that provides competitive advantage, as defined earlier.

15   In addition, there is a simple yet powerful validity check for the model. If the model behavior differs from the reference behavior pattern, either: (1) the team learned something they did not understand about the dynamic complexity surrounding the resource accumulation; or (2) the Key Resource Dynamics is modeled incompletely.

16   In thinking about strategy, we find it helpful to use the term resources instead of stocks, so that is what we will use throughout this book.

17   See HPS (2000).

18   'Net effect' resource stability analysis is a graphical representation of linear stability analysis. See Strogatz (1994) for a mathematical treatment of linear stability analysis.

19   Some readers will recognize this 'limits to growth' archetype as the logistics equation, where the population grows until it reaches the environment's carrying capacity.

20   From linear stability analysis the derivative (slope) of the net flow at the fixed point determines its stability. A positive slope is unstable and a negative slope is stable. See Strogatz (1994) for a straightforward mathematical derivation.

Chapter 6

1   See Barlas (1989), Forrester and Senge (1980), and Sterman (1987).

2   This is a variation on 'form follows function,' a famous saying in architectural design.

3   See Forrester (1982); Kampmann (1992); Mojtahedzadeh (1997); and Richardson (1995).

4   For an in-depth discussion of path loop dominance, see research presented in the *System Dynamics Review* by Mojtahedzadeh (1997); and Richardson (1995).

Chapter 7

1   We are indebted to Jay Forrest, a futurist with whom we have worked extensively, for helping structure our thinking in this section. For more of Jay's environmental scanning and research in studies of the future, see http://www.jayforrest.com/

Chapter 8

1   Argyris (1985) defined 'double-loop learning.'

2   See Forrest (1995).

Chapter 9

1   See Kaplan and Norton (1996, 65; 2000).

2   We have worked with Kaplan and Norton to apply system dynamics to Balanced Scorecard projects with clients in leading organizations. An example of our work is cited in Kaplan and Norton's book *The Strategy-Focused Organization* (Kaplan and Norton, 2000, 311–313).

3   See the book's website to see examples of these Balanced Scorecard learning environments. We provide links to the leading software companies that have developed the system dynamics modeling software and the enterprise management systems. We also provide a link to our research and curriculum development related to the benefits of using the Balanced Scorecard within an enterprise system.

4   BATNA stands for the Best Alternative To a Negotiated Agreement (Fisher, Ury, and Patton, 1991).

5   See Fisher, Ury, and Patton (1991); and Raiffa (1985).

6   *Oxford English Dictionary*, on-line version

7   See Keeney (1992); and Raiffa (1985).

8   See Ehrbar (1998).

9   NPV stands for Net Present Value.

10   See Collis and Montgomery (1998).

11   We thank Guillermo Babatz for insightful guidance in the development of our thinking about the roles and purpose of the corporate function.

12   See Brown and Eisenhardt (1998).

Chapter 10

1   See Manzoni and Barsoux (1998).

References

Andersen, D.F. and G.P. Richardson. 1997. Scripts for Model Building. *System Dynamics Review* **13**(2): 107–129.

Andrews, K. 1971. *The Concept of Corporate Strategy*. Homewood, IL: Irwin.

Argyris, C. 1985. *Strategy, Change, and Defensive Routines*. Boston: Pitman.

Argyris, C. 1993. *Knowledge for Action*. San Francisco: Jossey-Bass.

Arrow, K. 1974. The *Limits of Organizations*. New York: W.W. Norton and Company.

Barlas, Y. 1989. Multiple Tests for Validation of System Dynamics Type of Simulation Models. *European Journal of Operational Research* **42**: 59–87.

Barnard, C.I. 1968. *The Functions of the Executive*. Thirtieth Anniversary edn. Cambridge, MA: Harvard University Press.

Brown, S.L. and K.M. Eisenhardt. 1998. *Competing on the Edge: Strategy as Structured Chaos*. Cambridge, MA: Harvard Business School Press.

Collis, D.J. and C.A. Montgomery. 1998. *Corporate Strategy: A Resource-Based Approach*. Boston: Irwin McGraw-Hill.

Conner, K. 1991. A Historical Comparison of Resource-Based Theory and Five Schools of Thought within Industrial Organizational Economics: Do We Have New Theory of the Firm? *Journal of Management* **17**: 121–154.

Dierickx, I. and K. Cool. 1989. Asset Stock Accumulation and Sustainability of Competitive Advantage. *Management Science* **35**(12): 1504–1511.

Dupperin, J.C. and M. Godet. 1975. SMIC 74: A Method for Constructing and Ranking Scenarios. *Futures* 7(4): 302–312.

Duval, A., A. Fontela and A. Gabus. 1975. Cross-Impact Analysis: A Handbook on Concepts and Applications. In *Portraits of Complexity: Applications of Systems Methodologies to Societal Problems*, edited by M.M. Baldwin. Columbus, Ohio: Battelle.

Ehrbar, A. 1998. *EVA: The Real Key to Creating Wealth*. New York: John Wiley & Sons, Inc.

Fisher, R., W. Ury and B. Patton. 1991. *Getting to Yes: Negotiating Agreement Without Giving In*. New York: Penguin USA.

Forrest, J. 1995. *The Outlook For Simulation And Gaming In Management Training* [cited 1999]. Available from http://www.jayforrest.com/.

Forrester, J.W. 1961. *Industrial Dynamics*. Cambridge MA: Productivity Press.

Forrester, J.W. 1990. *Principles of Systems*. Portland, OR: Productivity Press.

Forrester, J.W. and P.M. Senge, eds. 1980. Tests for Building Confidence in System Dynamics Models. Edited by A. Legasto, J. W. Forrester and J. Lyneis. Vol. 14, *System Dynamics. TIMS Studies in the Management Sciences*. New York: North-Holland.

Forrester, N.B. 1982. A Dynamic Synthesis of Basic Macroeconomic Theory: Implications for Stabilization Policy Analysis. PhD, MIT, Cambridge.

Georgantzas, N.C. and W. Acar. 1995. Scenario-Driven Planning: Learning to Manage Strategic Uncertainty. Westport, CT: Quorum.

Glucksman, M., E. Mollona and J. Morecroft. 1997. Leapfrogging the Competition: The Dynamics of Resource Metamorphosis. Paper presented at 15th International System Dynamics Conference, at Istanbul.

Goodman, M.R. 1974. *Study Notes in System Dynamics*. Cambridge MA: Productivity Press.

Gouillart, F. and J. Kelly. 1995. *Transforming the Organization*. New York: McGraw-Hill.

Holmstrom, B. and J. Tirole. 1989. The Theory of the Firm. In *Handbook of Industrial Organization*, edited by R. Schmalensee and R. Willig. Amsterdam: North-Holland.

HPS. 2000. *An Introduction to Systems Thinking with ithink*. Hanover, NH: High Performance Systems.

Kampmann, C.E. 1992. Feedback Complexity and Market Adjustment: An Experimental Approach. Ph.D., M.I.T., Cambridge, MA.

Kaplan, R.S. and D.P. Norton. 1996. *The Balanced Scorecard: Translating Strategy into Action*. Cambridge, MA: Harvard Business School Press.

Kaplan, R.S. and D.P. Norton. 2000. *The Strategy-Focused Organization: How Balanced Scorecard Companies Thrive in the New Business Environment*. Cambridge, MA: Harvard Business School Press.

Keeney, R.L. 1992. *Value-Focused Thinking: A Path to Creative Decisionmaking*. Cambridge, MA: Harvard University Press.

Kelly, G.A. 1963. *A Theory of Personality*. New York: Norton.

Manzoni, J.-F. and J.-L. Barsoux. 1998. The Set-up-to-Fail Syndrome. *Harvard Business Review* **76**(2) 101–113.

Meadows, D. 1980. The Unavoidable A Priori. In *Elements of the System Dynamics Method*, edited by J. Randers. Cambridge, Mass: Productivity Press.

Mitchell, T.R. and W.S. Silver. 1990. Individual and Group Goals When Workers Are Interdependent: Effects on Task Strategies and Performance. *Journal of Applied Psychology* **75**: 185–193.

Mojtahedzadeh, M.T. 1997. A Path Not Taken: Computer Assisted Heuristics for Understanding Dynamic Systems. unpublished PhD dissertation, Department of Public Affairs and Policy, Rockefeller College, University of Albany, SUNY.

Morecroft, J. 1983. Concepts, Theory and Techniques: A Systems Perspective on Materials Requirement Planning. *Decision Sciences* **14**(1): 1–18.

Moxnes, E. 1998. Misperceptions of Bioeconomics. *Management Science* **44**(9): 1234–1248.

Nash, J.F. 1950. The Bargaining Problem. *Econometrica* **18**: 155–162.

Nonaka, I. and H. Takeuchi. 1995. *The Knowledge-Creating Company*. New York: Oxford University Press.

O'Leary-Kelly, A.M., J.J. Martocchio and D.D. Frink. 1994. A Review of the Influence of Group Goals on Group Performance. *Academy of Management Journal* **37**: 1285–1301.

Oshry, B. 1996. *Seeing Systems: Unlocking the Mysteries of Organizational Life*. San Francisco: Berrett-Koehler Publishers.

Quinn, J.B. 1980. *Strategies for Change: Logical Incrementalism*. Homewood, IL: Richard D. Irwin, Inc.

Radzicki, M.J. 1992. Dyadic Processes, Tempestuous Relationships and System Dynamics. *System Dynamics Review* **9**(1): 79–94.

Raiffa, H. 1985. *The Art and Science of Negotiation*. Cambridge, MA: Harvard University Press.

Richardson, G.P. 1991. *Feedback Thought in Social Science and Systems Theory*. Philadelphia: The University of Pennsylvania Press.

Richardson, G.P. 1995. Loop Polarity, Loop Dominance and the Concept of Dominant Polarity. *System Dynamics Review* **11**(1): 67–88.

Richardson, G.P. and A.L. Pugh, III. 1981. *Introduction to System Dynamics Modeling with DYNAMO*. Cambridge MA: Productivity Press.

Ritchie-Dunham, J.L. 1997. Initiating Management Dialog with a Summary Presentation that Integrates Findings from Multiple SD Analytical Tools. Paper presented at 15th International System Dynamics Conference: 'Systems Approach to Learning and Education into the 21st Century ', at Istanbul, Turkey.

Ritchie-Dunham, J.L. 1999. Evaluating Epidemic Intervention Policies with Systems Thinking: A Case Study of Dengue Fever in Mexico. *System Dynamics Review* **15**(2): 119–138.

Ritchie-Dunham, J. and A. Membrillo. 1999. Breaking Down Functional Blinders: A Systemic View of the Organizational Map. *The Systems Thinker* **10**(10).

Ritchie-Dunham, J. and A. Membrillo. 2000. Reconciling Local and Global Goals: A Systemic View of the Organizational Map. *The Systems Thinker* **11**(2).

Roberts, N.H., D.F. Andersen, R.M. Deal, M.S. Grant and W.A. Shaffer. 1983. *Introduction to Computer Simulation: The System Dynamics Modeling Approach*. Reading, MA: Addison-Wesley.

Scott-Morgan, P. 1994. *Unwritten Rules of the Game*. New York: McGraw-Hill.

Senge, P. 1990. *The Fifth Discipline*. New York: Doubleday Currency.

Simon, H.A. 1997. *Administrative Behavior*. 4th ed. New York: Free Press.

Smith, G.F. 1989. Defining Managerial Problems: A Framework for Prescriptive Theorizing. *Management Science* **35**(8): 963–981.

Sterman, J.D. 1987. Testing Behavioral Simulation Models by Direct Experiment. *Management Science* **33**(12): 1572–1592.

Sterman, J.D. 1991. The Skeptic's Guide to Computer Models. In *Managing a Nation: The Microcomputer Software Catalog*, edited by G.O. e. a. Barney. Boulder, CO: Westview Press.

Sterman, J.D. 2000. *Business Dynamics: Systems Thinking and Modeling for a Complex World*. Boston: Irwin McGraw-Hill.

Strogatz, S. 1994. *Nonlinear Dynamics and Chaos*. New York: Addison-Wesley.

Ven, A.H.V.d. 1987. Four Requirements for Processual Analysis. In *The Management of Change*, edited by A.M. Pettigrew. Oxford: Basil Blackwell.

Vennix, J. 1996. *Group Model Building: Facilitating Team Learning Using System Dynamics*. New York: Wiley.

Warren, K. 1997. Building Resources for Competitive Advantage. In *Mastering Management*. London: FT Pitman Publishing.

Wernerfelt, B. 1984. A Resource-Based View of the Firm. *Strategic Management Journal* (5): 171–180.

Index